All About Poetry Ideas

The South & South West

Edited by
Helen Davies

This book belongs to

First published in Great Britain in 2010 by

Remus House
Coltsfoot Drive
Peterborough
PE2 9JX
Telephone: 01733 890066
Website: www.youngwriters.co.uk

All Rights Reserved
Book Design by Spencer Hart
© Copyright Contributors 2010
SB ISBN 978-0-85739-164-3

Foreword

At Young Writers our defining aim is to promote an enjoyment of reading and writing amongst children and young adults. By giving aspiring poets the opportunity to see their work in print, their love of the written word as well as confidence in their own abilities has the chance to blossom.

Our latest competition *Poetry Express* was designed to introduce primary school children to the wonders of creative expression. They were given free reign to write on any theme and in any style, thus encouraging them to use and explore a variety of different poetic forms.

We are proud to present the resulting collection of regional anthologies which are an excellent showcase of young writing talent. With such a diverse range of entries received, the selection process was difficult yet very rewarding.

From comical rhymes to poignant verses, there is plenty to entertain and inspire within these pages. We hope you agree that this collection bursting with imagination is one to treasure.

Contents

Arian Moore (8) 1

Broughton Fields Primary School, Milton Keynes
Callum Jones & Jamal Fakhrou (11) 1
Farhi Chudha (11) 2
Hannah Victor (11) 2
Amber Brunson-Wilson (11) 3
Folabo Agunbiade (11) 3
Brandon Bloice (11) 4
William Bowen (10) 4
Brooke Perry (11) 5

Calder House School, Colerne
Alex Watson (10) 5
Sam Caple (10) 6
Lucas Reynolds (10) 6
James Payne (10) 7
Kyle Stevens (12) 7
Elliott Hawtin (11) 8
Jamie Rose (10) 9
Ffion King (11) 10

Hertsmere Jewish Primary School, Radlett
Adam Landau (11) 10
Simmy Wahnon (11) 11
Natalie Miller (11) 12
Gemma Rodol (10) 14
Rachel Scott (10) 15
Felicity Ginsburg (11) 16
Sophie Album (11) 17
Sam Karet (10) 18
Ben Rosen (10) 19
Zac Bloohn (11) 20
Gemma Levy (10) 21
Joshua Gruneberg (11) 21
Joshua Foreman (10) 22
Mia Bogush (10) 23
Chloe Gold (11) 23
Joshua Ross (10) 24
Lara Ziff (11) 24
Joshua Hermon (11) 25

Hillside First School, Verwood
Jordan Groves (9) 25
Jade Levett (9) 26
Jed Bartlett (9) 26
Anna Parnum (8) 27
Lauren Hawkins (9) 27
Amelia Gregory (8) 28
Jake Killgallon (9) 28

Kingsleigh Primary School, Bournemouth
Frankie Fisher (9) 28
Stacey Andrews (9) 29
Jade Pope (9) 30
Leah Lacey (9) 30
Caitlin Cooper (8) 31
Rebecca Spiers (8) 31
Craig Wright-Phillips (9) 32
Katrina Clegg (9) 32
Peter Lynch (9) 33
Richard Johns (9) 33
Katerina Sadry-Cade (9) 34
Georgia Phillips (9) 34
Jordan Hansford 34
Emily Oates (9) 35
Danielle Dunning (9) 35
Jade Eley (9) 35
Jack Twamley (9) 36
Martin Head (8) 36
Charlotte Bush (9) 36
Jason West (9) 36
Amarilla Antal (8) 37
Zack Cummings (9) 37

Linslade Lower School, Leighton Buzzard
Katie White (8) 37
Frankie Stewart (8) 38
Harry Worden (8) 39
Nayt Calvert (7) 39
Hana Benaceur (8) 39
Mark Boyle (8) 40

Amber Warren (7) 40
Louise Hammond (8) 40
Amy Marchant (8) 41
Ben Gilroy (8) 41
Murray McBoyle (8) 41
Kelley Picton (8) 41
Jessica Mound (8) 42

Malden Parochial CE Primary School, Worcester Park
Elise Evans (9) 42
Thomas Santini (9) 43
Ewan Grant (8) 43
Rory Airth (8) 44
Katherine Cunningham (9) 44
Sam Thomas (9) 45
Joshua Aruldragasam (9) 45
Maria O'Hagan (9) 46
William Taylor (9) 46
Charlotte Josey (8) 47
Camille Burfield (9) 47
Harry Krzystyniak (9) 48
Jack Alexander (9) 48
Isabelle Taylor (9) 49
Rebecca Davis (9) 49
Rachel Fathers (9) 49
Constandina Flouris (9) 50
Robin Barrington (9) 50
Danielle Holland (9) 50
Hannah Roberts (9) 51
Amelia Young (9) 51

Parish Church Junior School, Croydon
Abbey Grant (10) 51
Kirsty Northwood (11) 52
Tayla Danaher (10) 53
Oliver Sharp (11) 54
Elizabeth Petts (10) 55
Sadari Holness (10) 56
Maria Lenders (10) 57
Samuel Hayes (10) 58
Savannah Simmons (9) 58
Nana Addo-Kufuor (11) 59
Beatrix McCrae (8) 59
Joshua Bastock (10) 60
Ella Smoker (8) 60
Ella Dunn (10) 61

Deja Hutchison (10) 61
Michael Mensah (11) 62
Bonita Fearon (9) 62
Benjamin Fifield (10) 63
Tariq Shakur Badshah (8) 63
Laura Stoneham (9) 64
Tom Brunswick (9) 64
Amber Atouguia (10) 65
Liah Danquah (8) 65
Hana Shafieyfard (10) 66
James Moore (10) 66
Deepesh Rajeshkumar Patel (9) 67
Faith Gomez (10) 67
Shaneace Brown (10) 68
Anna Lofmark (8) 68
Joy Cummings (10) 69
Lakshana Sankar (8) 69
Molly Bielecki (7) 70
Levi Foka (10) 70
Harishon Sasikaran (11) 71
Phoebe Russell (7) 71
Shafiq Salahudeen (10) 72
Ross Maitland-Harris (10) 72
Sade Williams (10) 73
Shaquil Boakye (10) 73
Lana Headley (11) 74
Alice Ardis (8) 74
Khadijah Hayden (11) 75
Joel Akaje-Macauley (9) 75
Ope Oso (7) 76
Elise Marston (9) 76
Kerris Redway (10) 77
Jerelm Rose-Clarke (10) 77
Natasha Fearon (11) 78
Tina Bosa Bonsu (8) 78
Megan Elliott (8) 78
Libby Norton (8) 79
Samuel Oliver-Rowland (10) 79
Leah Terry (8) 79
Lauren Hawkes (7) 80
Thomas Smolen (8) 80
Emma Grummitt (8) 80
Dénae Chung (8) 81
Ryan Crockett (7) 81
Ellie-Dawn Wenham (8) 81
Edwina Ansong (8) 82
Natalie Ayim-Owusu (11) 82
Ayanna Korsah (9) 82

Riverside Primary School, London
Katherine Zuleta Gil (9) 83
Ryan Lieu (10) 83
Francis Kanneh (11) 84
Alma Crasmaru (11) 84
Daniela Monteiro (10) 85
Kitty Widdows (10) 85
Georgie Howell (10) 86
Blessing Aroboto (10) 86
Lisa Bushby (10) 87
Anita Milton-Hunter (10) 87
Ibraheem Keshinro (10) 88
Zayn Ali (10) 88
Ryan Sexton (11) 89
Ibrahim Doumbia (11) 89
Alexander Melnikov (10) 90
Blessing Kingston (9) 90
Damilula Odumusi (11) 91
Megan Lynch (9) 91
Mercedese Roach (10) 91
Rachael Fagbodun (9) 92
Alfie Butler (10) 92
Sophia Wahidullah (10) 92
Kheira Stambouli (9) 93
Kacie Ervin (9) 93
Harry Bradley (9) 93

St John's CE Primary School, Wellington
Jaimie Osborne (9) 94
Megan Blest (10) 95
Ellys Webb (7) 95
Kian Stafford (10) 96
Madison Davey (8) 96
Shannon Nutkins (10) 97
Jaime-Leigh Napper (9) 97
Lauren Thorne (11) 98
Sharnie Jenkins (11) 98
Benjamin Williams (8) 99
Robin Provis (8) 99
Simon Hollis (9) 99
Bethany Jade Fox (8) 100
Andrew Hollis & Tyler Wilkinson (11) .. 100
Leah Osborne (7) 100
James Eva (7) 101
Connor Cole (8) 101
Megan White (8) 101
Sophie Ward (11) 102

Evie Knight (7) 102
Reece Webber (8) 102
Jack Mason (7) 103
Amy Thorne (7) 103

St Peter's CE (VC) Junior School, Marlborough
Billy Millar (8) 103
Rohan Ball (9) 104
Harriet Thatcher (11) 105
Michael De Val (11) 106
Joseph Fillis (8) 107
Oesa Astley (7) 107
Zoe Hammond (9) 108
Emily Heard (11) 108
Thomas Padfield (11) 109
Mathew Hogg (11) 109
India Bloomfield (8) 110
Ethan Payne (9) 110
Aaron O'Connell (8) 111
Harvey Millar (11) 111
Talia Lovell-Clelford (9) 112
Becky Slade (11) 112
Andrew Boothman (11) 113
Dylan Barnes (7) 113
Roman Argent (8) 114
Daynah Owen (10)
& Paige Phillips (11) 114
Cameron Davies (11) 115
Vita Linnane (8) 115
Iwan Parry-Evans (11) 116

Sheddingdean Community Primary School, Burgess Hill
Hannah Chapman (9) 116
Jessica Green (11) 117
Tayla Lay (10) 118
Curtis Pummell (10) 119
Hannah Elston (9) 120
Kelly Blamire (11) 121
Jade Conticelli (10) 122
Hollie Steward (10) 123
Elysia Paine (10) 124
Joseph Anderson (10) 125
Hannah Goldsmith (10) 126
Jamie Bowles (11) 126
Blake Hayes (10) 127
Katie Watson (9) 127

Ben Docherty (10) 128
Bradley Birch (9) 128
Ollie Gregory (9) 129
Jack Heckels & Justin Smith (11) 129
Charlotte Ingleton (10) 130
Thomas Booth (10) 131
Sammy Smith (10) 132
Toby Wardrobe (10) 133
Sean Mallin (8) 134
Siân Johnston (9) 134
Sarah Chapman (8) 135
Prissy Parker (10) 135
Emily Parsons (8) 136
Adam Tubbs (8) 136
Joshua Plank (9) 137
Charlotte Brown (8) 137
Bryony Tarrant (9) 138
Owain McLoughlin (11) 138
Jaime Pink (10) 139
Paige Walker-Pettit (10) 139

The Queen Anne Royal Free CE (C) First School, Windsor
Hana-Jo Chester (9) 140
Premleen Kaur Virdi (8) 141
Daniel Wren 141

The Stoke Poges School, Slough
Isobel Gatehouse (11) 142
Reah Mann (10) 142
Idris Hussain (10) 143
Ethan Relf (10) 143
Aais Bukhari (8) 143
Saba Iqbal (8) 144
Cameron David (11) 144
Charlotte Ashley (8) 144
Suzilah Chowdhary (8) 145
Daniel Nankivell (11) 145
Emily Shieldhouse (7) 145
Gurneet Brar (11) 146
Gionluca Mallia (11) 146
Sabah Mahmood (8) 146
Anastasia Bergman (7) 147
Ethan Short (8) 147
Tayyib Fazal (8) 147
Ismail Mehmood (8) 148

The Poems

Happiness

Happiness is yellow like the warm summer's sun,
It tastes delicious like a bowl of strawberries and cream,
It smells like scented spring flowers ready to bloom.
Happiness looks like a meadow of green, wavy grass
and delicate flowers,
It sounds like birds chirping the dawn chorus,
It feels like warm, fluffy candyfloss.

Arian Moore (8)

Fernando Torres

Super Spanish skills,
Dancing around dressed in red,
Scores special goals with his head.

Super Spanish skills,
Fabulously fast,
Good celebrations and lovely dance.

Super Spanish skills,
Blistering pace
With booming shots.

Super Spanish skills,
He is so good,
He frightens teams a lot.

Super Spanish skills,
He can make the net rip
And skill up Chelsea
With one hand behind his hip!

Callum Jones & Jamal Fakhrou (11)
Broughton Fields Primary School, Milton Keynes

Water Attack!

Water is smooth
With a motion
It is so strange
Like the ocean

Children play there
They splish and splash
The waves jump up
And then they crash

The water is warm
They love to swim
It splashes wet
As they jump in

They see a fin
Oh no! Help, quick
They need a hand
They feel so sick.

Farhi Chudha (11)
Broughton Fields Primary School, Milton Keynes

Day At The Beach

I was inside a shark
And it was very dark.

I splashed
And crashed.

The sea was blue,
I was stuck like glue.

I made it to the coast
And was ready for my roast.

Hannah Victor (11)
Broughton Fields Primary School, Milton Keynes

I Rode Like A Cheetah

I ran through the forest
I ran through the wood
The dogs were pounding
As fast as they could
'I rode like a cheetah!'

The horse was running
As fast as lightning
The dogs were still chasing
It was very frightening
'I rode like a cheetah!'

I got away finally
The dogs had stopped
We were both panting
We both went and dropped
'I rode like a cheetah!'

Amber Brunson-Wilson (11)
Broughton Fields Primary School, Milton Keynes

Amazing Drogba

Astonishing African skills
Hungry for goals
Astonishing African skills
He slides and glides
Astonishing African skills
His exciting energy
Astonishing African skills
His hard, historic headers
Astonishing African skills
The dazzling Drogba
Astonishing African skills
He's dribbling Drogba.

Folabo Agunbiade (11)
Broughton Fields Primary School, Milton Keynes

All Aboard the Poetry Express

Fun, Fast Football

Fun, fast football,
What a cool match.
Fun, fast football,
What a great catch.

Fun, fast football,
What a great goal.
Fun, fast football,
And a big fall.

Fun, fast football,
Noisy people in the cold.
Run fast football,
A noisy, noisy day!

Brandon Bloice (11)
Broughton Fields Primary School, Milton Keynes

The Sea And Me

I love the sea because it's me,
I think it's my key.

My mind goes round and round
As I lie on the ground.

The smooth, silky sand is on my hand.
I can see some land across the sea, with a man.

William Bowen (10)
Broughton Fields Primary School, Milton Keynes

The Sea

The sea swishes from side to side,
The sea travels at any time,
Splish, splash, the children say,
Wise old sea come out to play.

Brooke Perry (11)
Broughton Fields Primary School, Milton Keynes

The Dream That Went Wrong

I awoke - he was coming!
Ran down the spiral stairs,
Faster and faster!
A sudden scream alerted me.
I looked up and saw him!
An alien, clad in armour plating,
Roaring, with two mouths,
One inside the other.
I screamed!
But he pounced,
His bloodshot eyes as red as Hell,
His black body slimy with oil
And claws as sharp as flints.
He ran at me,
Faster and faster,
His claws tapping on the floor!

Then I woke up
And he was gone.
Thank God!

Alex Watson (10)
Calder House School, Colerne

The Nightmare Begins!

I was walking through the fog
And then I saw him.
That dark silhouette tormenting me!
And then he walked towards me,
Closer and closer!
His hair greasy as butter,
His legs supple as a jaguar.
I dropped my bags!
I turned to run!
But he held me down,
His mouth slimy as a slug.
He raised his hand . . . *rrrring* . . . *rrrring*.
'Sam, breakfast's ready!'
It was only a dream!
The doorbell rang,
I went downstairs and opened it.
It was that man!
'I'm back!'

Sam Caple (10)
Calder House School, Colerne

The Dark Man

Sitting on my chair I heard a noise,
The upstairs bedroom door slammed.
Getting up, I went to the stairs
And there he was.
Standing on the top stair,
His eyes as green as emeralds,
His hair as thin as grass,
Dressed in a black suit.
He came towards me
So I hid.

Lucas Reynolds (10)
Calder House School, Colerne

Trenches

I sit on the firing step, wet and cold,
With my rifle in my hands,
Heavy as lead.
My feet are rotting in my boots,
It stinks like a sewer.
I can smell rotting flesh
And see rats running through the mud.
Tomorrow I'm going over the top!
Will I die or will I survive?

Today I'm going over the top.
Today I will find out
If I die or not.
The whistle blows,
I scramble over,
And when I get up
I walk towards my fate.

James Payne (10)
Calder House School, Colerne

Lightning

Lightning flies through the air like a dart,
Like an eagle searching for its prey.
Lightning is terrifying.
He kills every move he makes.
Buildings turn to dust!
He shines brightly
As he flies through the valleys,
Glistening gold,
Like a knight in shining armour.

Kyle Stevens (12)
Calder House School, Colerne

Trench Warfare

You start in the support trench,
Waiting for the call . . .
It comes with a burden.
As I walk towards the front line
I can imagine bullets piercing my skin.
I climb in, and what a beastly hell-hole!

I walk along the trench,
Mud gripping my legs with its stranglehold.
The order is given for the gunners to fire,
They are being picked off one by one.
Then the whistle blows.
I find myself running across no-man's-land!
All around me, bodies scattered,
As Death glides across like a feather in the wind,
And I know that my time may come.

Elliott Hawtin (11)
Calder House School, Colerne

Nightmare

Sitting in my chair
I heard a noise.
In front of me he stood,
Glaring!
His eyes as red as rubies,
With a dagger sharp as a razor!
I slammed the door,
I tried to barricade it
But . . .
It was too late!
He flew towards me like a comet,
His red cloak shining in the moonlight.
He tried to grab me
With hands as quick as a wizard,
But he missed!

Jamie Rose (10)
Calder House School, Colerne

Snow

She drifts through my garden,
Sweet as silk,
Covering everything white as sugar.
She moves gently,
Like a soft breeze.
Her dress dances like
Delicate snowflakes.
You can see icicles
Twinkling as she glides.
She settles down to sleep
In my garden,
Changing everything
Into a white world.

Ffion King (11)
Calder House School, Colerne

Goodbye Poem

When I saw my reflection through the colossal window
I held my mum's hand screaming, 'No, no, no, no!'
Then I stepped through the building seeing a smile on children's faces
They went to the hall to say their daily graces.

Then before I could pass I looked up, there she stood,
A smile on the head teacher, I hid under my hood.
I was scared as I didn't know anyone here,
I was trembling more than ever, I had much to fear.

Mrs Bazak created a spiritual atmosphere
And all I had done was just worriedly appear.
I'm so glad that I came through those big doors,
Now Mrs Bazak is leaving us from our school floors.

Adam Landau (11)
Hertsmere Jewish Primary School, Radlett

Goodbye Mrs Bazak

I looked up at the huge green door,
The huge green door looked back.
It seemed to stare at me
Through windows, which were black.
The strange face appeared to say,
'Come in for lots of fun today!'
And encouraged me on my way,
So over the threshold I went.

Inside was an encouraging smile
That helped me on my way,
A friendly voice that welcomed me
And bade my parents good day.
'Hello, I'm Mrs Bazak, head teacher here,
I'll guide you till your very last year.
Now off you go, your classroom is near.'
So off I quickly sped.

What followed were eight years
Of effort, learning and fun,
And every step of the way,
Mrs Bazak guided us on.
From watching her give out rewards
To children who kept to the laws,
Talking to people from Years 2, 3 and 4,
Kept us all on the straight and narrow.

Now we'll all be sad to see her go,
She's helped our school on its way,
She's been expertly guiding it
Since its very first day.
When she goes it will be sad,
But what she's done makes us feel glad.
It's been fun with her around.
Goodbye Mrs Bazak!

Simmy Wahnon (11)
Hertsmere Jewish Primary School, Radlett

How Sad We Are That You're Leaving

Our school head is leaving,
We are all very sad,
Everyone's heavily breathing
And going exceptionally mad!

'Who's going to come as head?' people say.
'They won't be better than Mrs Bazak,' I explain,
'I know they won't, even if you pray!'
'Mrs Bazak is great!' loudly shouts Wayne.

Our school head is leaving,
We're all very sad,
Everyone's heavily breathing,
And going exceptionally mad!

You've made this school a palace,
Something new every day,
Everything is accomplished
And amazing all the way.

Our school head is leaving,
We are all very sad,
Everyone's heavily breathing
And going exceptionally mad!

Garden, shelter, one extra class,
Astroturf, more PE and long green grass,
Everything has been a success,
All thanks to you, it's never a mess!

Our school head is leaving,
We are all very sad,
Everyone's heavily breathing
And going exceptionally mad!

You're very funny
And help everyone a lot,
Personality's very sunny,
Everything's a shot.

Our school head is leaving,
We are all very sad,
Everyone's heavily breathing
And going exceptionally mad!

Our school life has grown
Every day of our lives,
When we wake up, we never moan,
Even in the car when our parents drive.

Our school head is leaving,
We are all very sad,
Everyone's heavily breathing
And going exceptionally mad!

Now you are going,
Everything is changing,
Life is slowing
And stuff is rearranging.

Thanks for everything in this school,
It's been the best one yet,
We hope you have a great end life,
One you'll never forget.

Natalie Miller (11)
Hertsmere Jewish Primary School, Radlett

My Years And Yours

As I saw her dazzling smile
I walked away, just a few miles.
I could still feel the warmth in my body,
I still felt it while watching Noddy.

As I walked through the classroom door,
I was so very near the soft blue floor.
You were so tall and full of might,
Even taller than a flying kite.

In Year 1
It was very exciting, fun,
Learning all my ABC,
You really helped me.

In Year 2,
We saw cows in a field moo.
As I sat by your large brown door,
I felt very stupid and poor.

In Year 3
Was my first SATs test, whoopee.
As I sat in my chair
I thought that you were very fair.

In Year 4,
We learnt so much more.
I finally learnt about my teeth,
I went on about them in Bushey Heath.

In Year 5
I really felt like I thrived.
Next year was SATs,
So I put on my thinking cap.

I'm in my final year
And I have a very big fear.
In my new school
I don't want to be like a fool.

I know this won't be true,
Because of you.
You made me strong and clever,
You made sure I didn't say never.

We all might cry
When we say goodbye.
You've made school so great,
You have given me memories on a plate.

We will miss you,
You really are the very best,
Better than all the rest.
I will have a tear in my eye.
Will you, Mrs Bazak?

Gemma Rodol (10)
Hertsmere Jewish Primary School, Radlett

Smile

K ind Mrs Bazak and her helpfulness
I ncredible and hate-less
N aturally doing her patrolling
D irecting up and down the corridor, smiling

M rs Bazak has a beautiful smile
R unning down the corridor mile by mile
S miling back at her for a while

B ecause of her beautiful smile
A n angry expression can't settle on her face
Z apped her way downstairs at an easy pace
A s she entered the room examining
K indly sat down whilst smiling.

Rachel Scott (10)
Hertsmere Jewish Primary School, Radlett

Change

We were small and young,
Scared too,
As we stepped on the coach
To start something new.

Our mouths were parched,
Our throats felt tight,
As we entered through the gates
And stared up at the site.

This was it,
Our school to be,
A new adventure
Waiting for me.

We followed the others
Round the side
Of the towering building,
To be brave we tried.

In the playground we saw
All people our age,
We chatted a bit,
Then started to play.

Lesson time was fun,
We learnt all sorts,
We played outside
And enjoyed new sports.

As we moved up the school
Our fear went,
We were improving all round,
We found out what things meant.

We are the oldest now,
And we know a lot,
Our knowledge has expanded,
Scared anymore? We are not!

The end is nearing,
We will start a new school,
Our hearts filled with trepidation,
But we'll soon think it is cool!

Felicity Ginsburg (11)
Hertsmere Jewish Primary School, Radlett

What A Great Head Teacher You Are

Oh what a great head teacher you are,
I remember my first day at school,
Entering the large building
And walking into the hall.

Oh what a great head teacher you are,
The first time I met you
I spotted a huge smile on your face,
I admire you, it's true!

Oh what a great head teacher you are,
You have changed the school in so many ways
In my life from Nursery to Year 5,
And now in my Year 6 days.

Oh what a great head teacher you are,
I have learnt lots over the years,
The After SATs programme has been great,
So let's all stand up and say, 'Cheers!'

Oh what a great head teacher you are,
I really don't want you to go,
You have been inspiring for everyone,
But this is what you must know . . .

You truly are the best head teacher
I have or will ever come across!

Thank you.

Sophie Album (11)
Hertsmere Jewish Primary School, Radlett

An Era Of Happiness

Through the huge iron gates
All I could see was what looked like a big green house
With lots of windows and brick walls,
Which made me feel as small as a mouse.

When I saw that smiling face
I suddenly looked down at my shoelace.
The lady's voice said to me,
'Come on in, some students call me Mrs B.'

She said that Mrs Bazak was her name
And at the time I thought teaching was her game,
But it turned out that I was not very right,
A normal teacher's schedule would never be as tight.

When I found out,
She seemed quite cool,
Doing this and that,
Running the school.

Seven years have passed since that time,
And during that I have learnt to mime.
I have learnt plenty of other things too,
And she was there the whole time as I grew.

She will soon be leaving,
When she's sure to be crying,
As she will be missed by so many pupils like me,
And of her head teaching career, she will finally be free.

Sam Karet (10)
Hertsmere Jewish Primary School, Radlett

Our Years

There she stood,
Feeling good,
Mrs Bazak was her name,
As she said, 'Pick up your game.'

I've never been spoken to in a negative way,
Always positive - always encouragement as she will say,
Always smiles,
Spotting it for miles.

I never fear
While I'm in this spiritual atmosphere.
You can spot the atmosphere from the corner of your eye,
Whilst you're eating the school apple pie.

It's always a safe place,
When I see her bubbly face,
She is an inspiration to us all,
She will always be there if we call.

Year 6 has come,
Boy, I have had a lot of fun,
Outings, trips to all different places,
Especially meeting lots of new faces.

We will miss you!

Ben Rosen (10)
Hertsmere Jewish Primary School, Radlett

My Primary Days!

Just as I passed the school gates,
Mrs Bazak was there to wait,
There was a smile on her face,
But children were running with pace!

As I ran into the hall,
Everyone was having a ball.
Mrs Bazak suddenly arrived,
Then we all stopped!

Her smile was like the sun,
I was sure we were going to have a lot of fun.
As soon as I see her shining face,
She makes the school into a safer place!

My final day,
I say, 'Hip hip hooray,'
She waves goodbye,
I begin to sigh!

Mrs Bazak, you're truly the best,
I will never forget you
Because you're better than the rest!

Zac Bloohn (11)
Hertsmere Jewish Primary School, Radlett

What Will I Do Without You?

I went towards the huge green doors
Where she was standing with great applause.
I took my coat off and waved goodbye,
Trying very hard not to cry.

I could not believe I was here,
In the playground with no fear.
Standing straight when the whistle goes,
The new teaches come while the wind blows.

Mrs Bazak came in the hall
While we were all having a ball.
She didn't really shout - only softly spoke,
And I only just awoke.

Now I feel much more stronger
And have been at the school for so much longer,
I feel I will honestly miss you,
As much as the whole school too.

Goodbye Mrs Bazak.

Gemma Levy (10)
Hertsmere Jewish Primary School, Radlett

Mrs Bazak

M ost grateful for all you have done
R emember you because you have made
   my years in Hertsmere great
S ensitive to everyone you are

B est head teacher we've ever had
A mazing times you have given
Z ealous you are in your career
A dmirable you are to all
K een to work for HJPS.

Joshua Gruneberg (11)
Hertsmere Jewish Primary School, Radlett

Tear In Her Eye!

I stand in front of the big black gates,
I'm finally here, at last.
Mrs Bazak knows me well,
Now my years have passed.

  H ertsmere is the school I'm leaving
  J ewish education is a great thing we learn
  P iles of paperwork you no longer need to do as you
    are also leaving
  S o I can say I'm proud of myself because of the knowledge I earn

  M agical powers must belong to you
  R ight from the moment you got here
  S chools over the world must want you as their head

  B ecause you create such a special atmosphere

From the very last day of school,
I think I am going to cry,
But as Mrs B leaves the school,
Do you think she'll have a tear in her eye?

Joshua Foreman (10)
Hertsmere Jewish Primary School, Radlett

How Will We Say Goodbye?

How will we say goodbye?
You've done so much for us,
We won't be able to bear it!

How will we say goodbye?
You've been with us since nursery,
It has been such a fun time.

How will we say goodbye?
Wonderful lessons you have planned,
And the greatest teachers in the land!

How will we say goodbye?
You have always been so very kind
And have helped us come so far!

How will we say goodbye?
You have built the school up to be the best
And it is so much better than the rest!

Mia Bogush (10)
Hertsmere Jewish Primary School, Radlett

Farewell

My hands clenched together,
As I saw Mrs Bazak
My eyes were about to cry,
When I stepped in the foyer,
I could tell she was a smiley lady.

She has created a wonderful school for our education,
We have travelled far and far,
And now it's time to say bye-bye,
You are a wonderful head teacher,
I couldn't ask for a better one.

Chloe Gold (11)
Hertsmere Jewish Primary School, Radlett

Our School Head Teacher

The enormous school stood in front of me,
As I cautiously stepped up to the door,
I nervously walked inside,
And the spiritual atmosphere took me on a tour.

Mrs Bazak stood in front of me,
She guided me around the school
With her friendly face looking down at me.
Oh, I wish there was a pool.

I saw children smiling at me,
Making me feel part of the community.
For seven years I've been with my friends,
Thinking up lots of new trends.

Joshua Ross (10)
Hertsmere Jewish Primary School, Radlett

HJPS And Me

Wow! The gigantic building stares at me,
How excited and nervous I'll be.
I walk into school and see my friends smiling,
I never knew I wouldn't be crying.

I look forward to having an exciting day,
Whilst learning in an enjoyable way.
It's time for assembly, Mrs Bazak comes,
We're all so scared, we want our mums.

Years have passed, time to go,
Secondary school time for a show.
Mrs Bazak, what can we say?
You are the best in every way!

Lara Ziff (11)
Hertsmere Jewish Primary School, Radlett

Goodbye Mrs Bazak

Goodbye Mrs Bazak, you taught us
And we thank you for all we know
And know you're leaving to go.

I arrived in HJPS when I was four,
I had no clue what to do,
But you helped me with every step.

When I first entered HJPS
You ensured that I did well
And now it's time to say farewell.

Joshua Hermon (11)
Hertsmere Jewish Primary School, Radlett

Pink And Fluffy

I hate pink and fluffy things
They're just for girly girls!
People that wear heels and rings
And have their hair in curls.

I hate pink and sparkly stuff,
They make my skin crawl, they're not cool.
Things like that make my face puff,
Luckily all this stuff is not allowed at school!

People out in short dresses,
Fake tan and make-up files,
Having hair with waves and tresses
Makes me run for miles and miles!

Jordan Groves (9)
Hillside First School, Verwood

Haunted House

Tiptoe, tiptoe up to the front door,
Creaking silently as I open the door,
I hear snoring, I creep up the noisy stairs,
Oh no, there's a headless monster in there!
Ghosts are coming,
The cats are screeching,
The skeletons are dancing
And spiders are prancing,
Numbing up your body.
I run down the noisy stairs and out the door,
I'm never going there again.

Jade Levett (9)
Hillside First School, Verwood

The Haunted House

Once on Halloween, I went to the haunted house
But then it grave me the creeps.
Vampires going up to my face,
Argh! It was just a disgrace.
The zombies jumping out near my head,
Skeletons hanging and tripping me up - ow!
I'm about to cry.
Oh well, at least it's better than
Being about to die.

Jed Bartlett (9)
Hillside First School, Verwood

Climbing Time

I climb on the furniture
Then fall on my brother,
He screamed and cries, runs to bed,
Jumps in the shower,
Bangs his head.
He falls on the floor,
Trips over the sofa, cracks his head.
Oh dear, it's all my fault,
Maybe I should do some reading instead!

Anna Parnum (8)
Hillside First School, Verwood

Bad Thoughts

This is the biggest horse show of the year,
I don't know how to lose my fear.
What happens if it goes wrong?
I might gallop into the fence,
What will happen?
Will I lose a sense?
I might get eliminated.
'Don't worry, it's only a friendly,' says my mum.
'Help!' I say.

Lauren Hawkins (9)
Hillside First School, Verwood

The Time We Locked Our Sisters Out

When we locked our sisters outside,
We laughed our heads off
And ran away upstairs.
Our mum and dad said, 'Don't do that!'
But we did . . . we knew we were
Going to be in for it . . .
Because they didn't have any lunch . . . !

Amelia Gregory (8)
Hillside First School, Verwood

The Haunted House

Tiptoe, tiptoe, open that door,
Tiptoe, tiptoe, blood on the floor.
Look through the window, nothing there,
Open the door, there's a bed in there.
Argh! There's a headless man on the bed,
Is he alive? No, I think he's dead!

Jake Killgallon (9)
Hillside First School, Verwood

My Fat Old Cat

My cat can swing
My cat can sing
My cat can put stuff in the dustbin
My cat can swim
My cat can dance
My cat can go to France
My cat can eat
My cat has a very special seat
I have a very fat old cat.

Frankie Fisher (9)
Kingsleigh Primary School, Bournemouth

Dreams In Wonderland

Alice dreams
Of being confident.
A cookie dreams
Of being eaten.
A drink dreams
Of being drunk.
A queen of hearts dreams
Of being famous.
A flamingo dreams
Of standing upright.
A mushroom dreams
Of being eaten.
A dormouse dreams
Of having peace and quiet.
A white rabbit dreams
Of being on time.
A caterpillar dreams
Of being important.
A mad hatter dreams
Of being on stage.
A baby dreams
Of learning to walk.
A Cheshire cat dreams
Of being a normal person.
A hedgehog dreams
Of being tall and being brave.

Stacey Andrews (9)
Kingsleigh Primary School, Bournemouth

Dreams Of Wonderland

A white rabbit
Dreams of being on time.
A dark tunnel
Dreams of being light.
A bottle of juice
Dreams of being empty.
A chocolate chip biscuit
Dreams of being eaten.
A beautiful garden
Dreams of being run in.
A Cheshire cat
Dreams of being normal.
Tweedledum dreams
Of being Tweedledee.
A spiky hedgehog
Dreams of not being hit.
A pink fluffy flamingo
Dreams of not being stretched.

Jade Pope (9)
Kingsleigh Primary School, Bournemouth

Dreams Of Alice

A white rabbit dreams of being on time,
A beautiful garden dreams of being more beautiful,
A biscuit dreams of being delicious and making people taller,
A Cheshire cat dreams of a bowl of mice and a bowl of cream,
A bottle of potion dreams of making people drunk
And making people shrink,
A dark tunnel dreams of being dug up,
A sneezing pepper pot dreams of not sneezing.

Leah Lacey (9)
Kingsleigh Primary School, Bournemouth

Dreams In Wonderland

A Cheshire cat dreams
Of eating mice.

Alice dreams
Of being especially confident.

A white rabbit dreams
Of not losing his gloves.

A drink dreams
Of being sparkly.

A dormouse dreams
Of a feather bed.

A mad hatter dreams
Of singing better.

A queen of hearts dreams
Of slicing everybody's heads off.

Caitlin Cooper (8)
Kingsleigh Primary School, Bournemouth

Dreams In Wonderland

Alice dreams
Of being confident.

A white rabbit dreams
Of being on time.

A dormouse dreams
Of peace and quiet.

A tiger lily dreams
Of silence.

The knave of hearts dreams
Of not being accused of everything.

Rebecca Spiers (8)
Kingsleigh Primary School, Bournemouth

Dreams In Wonderland

Alice dreams
Of gaining confidence.

A white rabbit dreams
Of being on time.

A mad hatter dreams
Of having a proper tea party.

A queen of hearts dreams
Of heads being cut off all day.

A flamingo dreams
Of being the right way up.

A knave of hearts dreams
Of not being blamed all the time.

Craig Wright-Phillips (9)
Kingsleigh Primary School, Bournemouth

Dreams Of Wonderland

Alice dreams
Of becoming more confident,
Tweedledum and Tweedledee dream
Of fighting,
A queen of hearts dreams
Of jam tarts,
A white rabbit dreams
Of being on time,
A baby dreams
Of being pretty,
A duchess dreams
Of being nice,
A mad hatter dreams
Of a cup of tea.

Katrina Clegg (9)
Kingsleigh Primary School, Bournemouth

Dreams Of Wonderland

Alice dreams
Of being confident,
A dormouse dreams
Of a warm place to sleep,
A queen of hearts dreams
Of jam tarts,
A mad hatter dreams
Of singing well,
A king of hearts dreams
Of a quiet, slim, trim wife,
A flamingo dreams
Of the World Cup!

Peter Lynch (9)
Kingsleigh Primary School, Bournemouth

Dreams In Wonderland

A Cheshire cat dreams
Of stopping smiling.

A flamingo dreams
Of not being upside down.

A white rabbit dreams
Of being on time.

Alice dreams
Of being confident.

A dormouse dreams
Of getting peace and quiet.

Richard Johns (9)
Kingsleigh Primary School, Bournemouth

Dreams In Wonderland

Alice dreams
Of being more confident at singing

A white rabbit dreams
Of being on time

A door key dreams
Of not being turned and twisted
By people

Tweedledum and Tweedledee
Dream of being friends and
Playing together well.

Katerina Sadry-Cade (9)
Kingsleigh Primary School, Bournemouth

Dreams

A white rabbit dreams of being on time,
A pink flamingo dreams of flying free,
A white rose dreams of being red,
A grinning cat dreams of a warm fire and a bowl full of fish,
A queen dreams of screaming for hours,
A bottle of potion dreams of making people small,
A tortoise dreams of dancing around,
A lily dreams to be smelt.

Georgia Phillips (9)
Kingsleigh Primary School, Bournemouth

White Rabbit · Haiku

White Rabbit is late
Alice falls down the big hole
Into a weird land.

Jordan Hansford
Kingsleigh Primary School, Bournemouth

Dreams Of Alice

A Cheshire cat dreams of not grinning,
The beautiful garden dreams of the lovely red roses,
A white rabbit dreams of racing to get there on time,
A talking daisy dreams of singing out loud to everyone,
A biscuit dreams of not being eaten by somebody,
A dark tunnel dreams for people to walk through it.

Emily Oates (9)
Kingsleigh Primary School, Bournemouth

Dream Poem

A beautiful garden dreams of someone to visit,
A bottle of potion dreams of being drunk,
A yummy biscuit dreams of being eaten,
A dark tunnel dreams to be light,
A Cheshire cat dreams of being normal,
A white rabbit dreams of being on time.

Danielle Dunning (9)
Kingsleigh Primary School, Bournemouth

Jane In Jeans

Jane in jeans
Has jeans that are mean
And jeans that are as skinny as a mean bean
Her jeans are made of beans
And now her jeans are smelly and burnt.

Jade Eley (9)
Kingsleigh Primary School, Bournemouth

Dreams Of Alice - Haiku

The Queen of Hearts shouts,
'Off with his head!' she shouts loud
She is mad and nuts.

Jack Twamley (9)
Kingsleigh Primary School, Bournemouth

The Mad Hatter - Haiku

The Mad Hatter is
Mad as mad as mad can be
That's the Mad Hatter.

Martin Head (8)
Kingsleigh Primary School, Bournemouth

Bigger And Smaller Alice - Haiku

The pretty Alice
Grows bigger and much smaller
It is annoying.

Charlotte Bush (9)
Kingsleigh Primary School, Bournemouth

A Cup Of Nice Tea - Haiku

A cup of hot tea
It walks around so like me
Very nice indeed!

Jason West (9)
Kingsleigh Primary School, Bournemouth

Alice In The Garden - Haiku

Roses painted red
The angry queen chops off heads
Alice plays croquet.

Amarilla Antal (8)
Kingsleigh Primary School, Bournemouth

Sleepy - Haiku

A sleepy dormouse
Sleeps next to the Mad Hatter
And the March Hare too.

Zack Cummings (9)
Kingsleigh Primary School, Bournemouth

The Canal Boat

One day my daughter
Walked by the water.

I took a list
And I started to drift.

I have a mouse
Inside my canal house.

I bought a boat
And a coat.

I always like a stoat
And go around and around a moat.

I have a pet mole
And it looks like coal.

Katie White (8)
Linslade Lower School, Leighton Buzzard

Keep On Going

Keep on going,
Keep on pushing,
Although you want to stop.
Keep on going,
Keep on pushing,
I know it hurts a lot.
Keep on going,
Keep on pushing,
The dawn is breaking,
My back's aching.
Keep on going,
Keep on pushing,
One more mile,
I can see a stile.
Keep on going,
Keep on pushing
We're almost there,
Is that an imaginary hare?
Keep on going,
Keep on pushing,
It's dark but
We'll soon see the light.
Keep on going,
Keep on pushing,
We are here,
Let's celebrate with beer.

Frankie Stewart (8)
Linslade Lower School, Leighton Buzzard

I Like Drinking Canals

I like drinking canals,
Even though it's not so good.
The water is brown and dirty,
It does not taste like pud.

I like drinking canals,
They are dirty and very wet.
I like to suck it with a straw,
It's the yummiest thing yet.

Harry Worden (8)
Linslade Lower School, Leighton Buzzard

Leg It Boys

Leg it to light
Leg it to the other side
Leg it to the horse
Leg it or die
Leg it to survive
Leg it because you will survive
Be careful because maybe
The bridge will collapse.

Nayt Calvert (7)
Linslade Lower School, Leighton Buzzard

The Shiny Water - Haiku

The shiny water
And the waterfalls crashing
All day it does that.

When I sit watching
Watching all the water gleam
The rain falls on me!

Hana Benaceur (8)
Linslade Lower School, Leighton Buzzard

Navvies Acrostic

N avvies are as tough as tigers
A ll day long we work as hard as a logger
V iolent as a soldier
V icious as a rhino
I am a navvie
E very navvie is as clever as a parrot
S ee us navvies working so hard.

Mark Boyle (8)
Linslade Lower School, Leighton Buzzard

Horse

H orses are very strong so they can pull the boat along.
O n and on they pull the boat along.
R eins are attached to the horse.
S lowly the horse pulls the boat along.
E very canal boat has a horse pulling it.

Amber Warren (7)
Linslade Lower School, Leighton Buzzard

My Daughter

I pushed my daughter into the water,
She got very wet.
She coughed and spluttered
And angrily muttered,
I did it for a bet!

Louise Hammond (8)
Linslade Lower School, Leighton Buzzard

Sparkling Jugs

Jugs are colourful,
Bright and beautiful,
Gleaming through the moonlight,
The jugs all sparkle.

Amy Marchant (8)
Linslade Lower School, Leighton Buzzard

Green Lily Pads - Haiku

Green lily pads float
Frogs hop along blue water
Frogs hop on a log.

Ben Gilroy (8)
Linslade Lower School, Leighton Buzzard

Water Is Sodden - Haiku

Water is sodden
The blue reflection of light
Drip, drop, drip, drop, drip.

Murray McBoyle (8)
Linslade Lower School, Leighton Buzzard

Water - Haiku

Blue waves go *bash, splash!*
A showery day is cold.
Waterfalls go down.

Kelley Picton (8)
Linslade Lower School, Leighton Buzzard

Lilies On Water - Haiku

Lilies in water
Fish swim fast across water
Frogs hop and jump fast.

Jessica Mound (8)
Linslade Lower School, Leighton Buzzard

In My Garden . . .

In my garden I have . . .
Roses like rubies,
Buttercups like the sun
And tulips like lava.

In my garden I have . . .
Tomatoes as round as Earth,
Runner beans as big and juicy as a banana
And potatoes as yummy as chocolate.

In my garden I have . . .
Roses like rubies,
Buttercups like the sun
And tulips like lava.

In my garden I have . . .
Butterflies as fair as tissue paper,
Squirrels with tails as bushy as a feather duster
And a puppy as sweet as sugar.

In my garden I have . . .
Roses like rubies,
Buttercups like the sun
And tulips like lava.

Elise Evans (9)
Malden Parochial CE Primary School, Worcester Park

My Car Poem

In my car shop
I have Bentleys and Ferraris,
Lamborghinis, Maseratis,
I've got some Mercedes for some ladies
And Porsches for people with horses.

In my car shop
I've got Peugeots and Audis,
Which are great for big crowdies,
I've also got Toyotas,
But make sure they've all got motors.

In my car shop
I've got Citroens and Bugattis,
If you're not fond of taxis.
I've got Aston Martins and Rolls Royces,
You pay your money and make your choices.

Thomas Santini (9)
Malden Parochial CE Primary School, Worcester Park

Haunted House

H ouses are mostly normal, but this one isn't
A s soon as you go in, ghosts appear
U p above, bats screech a lot
N agging witches annoy you
T he children scream
E vil people might kill you
D ead bodies hanging up above

H aunted houses are so scary
O striches peck you
U sed sword with blood on it
S hiny armour attacks you
E vil books eat you.

Ewan Grant (8)
Malden Parochial CE Primary School, Worcester Park

The Animal Rap

Down deep in the jungle where the lion goes *roar,*
The animals fight over the meat in his jaw,
But it's always in the lion's jaw when he uses his mighty roar.
It's the animal rap, it's the animal rap.

Down deep in the jungle where the snake goes *hiss,*
He slithers through the jungle in disguise,
Sneaking up on people.
It's the animal rap, it's the animal rap.

Down deep in the jungle, the monkey goes *ooh, ooh,*
Swinging in the trees,
Flipping all around.
It's the animal rap, it's the animal rap.

Down deep in the jungle the animals make different sounds,
It's the animal rap, it's the animal rap.

Rory Airth (8)
Malden Parochial CE Primary School, Worcester Park

Zoo Disaster

In the zoo I can see
Hissing snakes,
Hippo lakes,
Hairy spiders,
Siberian tigers,
Tearing claws,
Mighty roars,
Scraping cages,
Children's ages,
Penguins catching,
Enclosures unlatching,
Children screaming,
Everybody leaving.

Katherine Cunningham (9)
Malden Parochial CE Primary School, Worcester Park

Dreams

In my dream I can see . . .
Angels flying,
Panthers dying,
Doves crying.

My dream has . . .
Tyrannosaurus-rex stomping,
Velociraptors jumping,
Gigantosaurus thumping.

My dream has . . .
Romans charging,
Ango-Saxons barging,
Vikings lying.

All in my dream.

Sam Thomas (9)
Malden Parochial CE Primary School, Worcester Park

A Haunted House

H aunted houses are very rare but they exist
A ghost appears as you come in
U nder the roof, bats screeching
N agging Natalie, the native, will annoy you
T he cackling children shouting
E vil flowers awakening with a big laugh
D otty dames jumping about crazily

H opping hooligans lurking around
O n top of the roof, a voice screaming
U gly dragons breathing fire
S illy blood-sucking vampires biting
E verything I have just told you about
    all happens in the haunted house!

Joshua Aruldragasam (9)
Malden Parochial CE Primary School, Worcester Park

Instruments

Cellos and violins,
Harps and violas,
Are all strings,
Instruments, instruments, instruments.

Piano,
Do it to the right tempo,
Keyboards too,
Instruments, instruments, instruments.

Tambourines and cymbals,
Castanets and drums,
These are all percussion,
Instruments, instruments, instruments.

Maria O'Hagan (9)
Malden Parochial CE Primary School, Worcester Park

Animals

Fat frogs leaping from lily pad to lily pad,
Fat frogs eating leaves, turning fat,
What are we going to do about that?
Fat frogs going *ribbet, ribbet,*
Don't smell his *ribbet,* it has too many leaves!

Small skunks doing smelly smells,
Don't scare him or he'll do that again.
Smelly skunks are very spiky,
So don't come too close.
Smelly skunks go home and have a nice sleep.

William Taylor (8)
Malden Parochial CE Primary School, Worcester Park

Haunted House

In the haunted house there is . . .
A skinny skeleton,
A kicking knight,
A pink pumpkin,
A super-squeaky door,
A whacked window,
A crackling candle,
A flaming fire,
A rocky rocking chair,
All in the haunted house.

Charlotte Josey (8)
Malden Parochial CE Primary School, Worcester Park

Living Things

Flowers are blooming,
Poppies are popping,
Bluebells are ringing,
Leaves are dropping,
Puppies are loving,
Tomatoes are boiling,
Grapes are peeling,
Mangoes are good
As a meteor.

Camille Burfield (9)
Malden Parochial CE Primary School, Worcester Park

Marvellous Monkey

Marvellous monkey swinging from the high trees,
Marvellous monkey having some lovely leaves,
Marvellous monkey eating a bunch of bananas,
Marvellous monkey coming to you, to yo-yo.

Marvellous monkey escape from the forest,
Marvellous monkey in the city,
Marvellous monkey at KFC mmm, yum, yum,
Marvellous monkey goes back home.

Harry Krzystyniak (9)
Malden Parochial CE Primary School, Worcester Park

Swirling Space

A planet in the sky,
Asteroids floating around,
While there is an alien eating a pie,
Stars making no sound.
Meteors hurtling towards Earth,
Space stations circling around,
While there is an alien having a surf,
Comets falling to the ground.

Jack Alexander (9)
Malden Parochial CE Primary School, Worcester Park

Pelican

The mighty pelican swoops down
Catches his fish, trying not to drown
As soon as he is flying high in the air
His hair stands on end
When he winds round the bend
And his beak starts to extend
As he winds round the bend
There that's the pelican!

Isabelle Taylor (9)
Malden Parochial CE Primary School, Worcester Park

Dreamland

Dreamland,
As soon as you put your head on the pillow
You are transported to this magical land
Where teddy bears live,
Playing in this beautiful palace and
The king of dreamland loves to hug his visitors.
There is strawberry jelly and marshmallows too,
But when you wake up, teddies are always happy.

Rebecca Davis (9)
Malden Parochial CE Primary School, Worcester Park

The Snail And Fred

There was a very big snail who left a very long trail,
He brushed his hair with a golden pear.
His best friend was Fred
And they both shared a bed in a giant shed,
Where they both became dead.
Now that is the end of the snail and Fred.

Rachel Fathers (9)
Malden Parochial CE Primary School, Worcester Park

Rap

Michael Jackson steps on the stage and
'Wow,' I say, 'it's the right page.'
Michael Jackson starts to sing Thriller
And I say he's the pop king.

JLS step on the stage and I say, 'Wahey!'
JLS start to dance,
Simon says they've got a chance.

Constandina Flouris (9)
Malden Parochial CE Primary School, Worcester Park

Weather

W hat will the weather be today?
E dge of London, raining all day
A ll around Kingston sunny until tomorrow
T here will be lots of sorrow.
H ail in Sussex
E ssex has showers and so does Wessex
R ain everywhere else not mentioned!

Robin Barrington (9)
Malden Parochial CE Primary School, Worcester Park

Friends

F orever together
R oughly playing
I n break
E very day
N ever breaking up
D oing
S ome bad fun.

Danielle Holland (9)
Malden Parochial CE Primary School, Worcester Park

In My Shop

In my shop I have . . .
Liquorice as black as a vampire's cape,
Strawberry creams as pink as lipstick,
Sherbet lemons as yellow as the sun,
Smarties as colourful as the rainbow
And a blackcurrant Starburst as purple as the sky!

Hannah Roberts (9)
Malden Parochial CE Primary School, Worcester Park

Pop Star Madness

Talented pop stars with clear voices,
Fans screaming, making noises,
Holding banners, eating popcorn,
Pushing through the crowd.
I feel dizzy.

Amelia Young (9)
Malden Parochial CE Primary School, Worcester Park

The Sun

The sun, the sun is as round as a bun,
When you learn about it it's lots of fun.
It burns and burns until it's all burned out!

The days pass and the days start
And the sun will still be there!
And people say, 'But *where?*'
From now, people need to care.

The sun, the sun is a ball of fire,
It's above the Earth and much, much higher!
Some of the facts are so amazing,
People say you're such a liar.

Abbey Grant (10)
Parish Church Junior School, Croydon

My Magic Box
(Based on 'Magic Box' by Kit Wright)

I will put in my box . . .
My emotion when I was first born,
My first cry,
My first little dream as I was asleep.

I will put in my box . . .
My first tooth coming through,
My first day going to preschool,
My first hug and love.

I will put in my box . . .
My first try of yummy baby food,
My whole family and fantastic friends,
My first step and word and laughter.

I will put in my box . . .
My favourite food,
My first day of infant school,
My first day of Parish Church Junior School.

My box is made of gold, silver and purple,
With pictures of me when I was a baby,
And secrets in the darkest of corners.
Its hinges are the claws of an eagle.

I shall remember everything that has happened in my life.
When I go to Heaven I will take the box with me.
I will travel in time with my box
And swim in the sea which is the same colour as the night sky.

Kirsty Northwood (11)
Parish Church Junior School, Croydon

Forests Are . . .

Forests are green,
Forests are bright,
Forests have many trees.
How many do they have?

100, 200? I don't know!

Forests are endless,
Forests are deflating,
Forests are in danger,
Why do people cut them down?
For more room, I suppose?

Forests are wild,
Forests are a home for wild animals,
Forests need help,
Forests have many animals,
Forests are being cut down,
People need to think,
Think about what?

People need to think before they do,
Before they do what?

Before they cut the trees down,
And think about what?

Think about the wild animals' homes
And habitats being . . .
Being destroyed.

Tayla Danaher (10)
Parish Church Junior School, Croydon

My Own Magic Box
(Based on 'Magic Box' by Kit Wright)

I will put in my box . . .
A Lego brick made of pure diamond,
A mango made of gold
And the eighth wonder of the world.

I will put in my box . . .
The last breath of a grandparent,
The last episode of a great TV programme
And the last sight of a good friend.

I will put in my box . . .
The first sight of a famous place,
My first ever friend
And the first competition I ever won.

I will put in my box . . .
My very first sentence,
The first game I ever made
And the first note of a piano.

My box will be made of thorns,
So that it will be intangible to everyone except me.
On each spike is a different dream
Waiting to be released.

In my box I will be like Peter Pan
And no one shall ever die.
In my box I will never be lonely.

Oliver Sharp (11)
Parish Church Junior School, Croydon

Not Scared Anymore

When I come home from school,
I fear my greatest fear,
If and when the bully
Will scarily appear.

I know it's kind of weak,
But bullying's against the rules.
I can't believe Mum when she tells me,
'Bullies are fools!'

I sometimes get quite angry,
Because I am always kind,
Even to the bully,
It makes me lose my mind!

I don't know why I get teased,
Maybe because of my weird hair.
I get really sad, you see,
When people laugh and stare.

My cheeks really hurt
When the bully gets violent with my face.
My jaw swells up purple
And I look a disgrace.

So now when I'm alone,
I'm usually in my room,
I walk home with friends now,
So I'm happy and in bloom!

Elizabeth Petts (10)
Parish Church Junior School, Croydon

Chocolate

Chocolate, chocolate in my mouth,
Yummy, scrumptious, I say, 'Wow!'
And it's like Heaven
And ice cream,
Brown as my skin,
Thick as my knee.

My friends say, 'Wow!'
My teachers say, 'Yummm,'
But I say, 'None.'

I come back from school
And my chocolate's gone!
I cry and cry,
I wonder why.
My mum says to me,
'I bet it's Dad,
He's really, really greedy.'
I ask him and ask him
But he says no.
That person's going to get payback
And they should know.
But then I see chocolate dots
On her face.
It's my mum,
It was a disgrace!
Why Mum!

Sadari Holness (10)
Parish Church Junior School, Croydon

Can I?

Can I?
Can I?
Can I do that?
Can I shout out loud?
Can I roll on the mat?

Can I feel your hair?
Can I see you as cool?
Can I make a jelly sandwich
And take it to school?

One day
We'll play
And say
Can I feed you poodle noodles?
Can I give the book a brand new look?
Can I make a wish for him to give me a kiss?
Can I put fruits in your boots?

Can I put tea in the sea
And hit a bear with a chair?
Can I eat a bun on the sun?
Can I make a rabbit have a habit?

Can I what?
Can I make a rabbit have a habit?
What kind of fool do you think I am?

Maria Lenders (10)
Parish Church Junior School, Croydon

I Could

I could be a crow,
I could be called Moe,
I could be called Fred,
I'd hide under your bed.

I could eat a frog,
I could drink out of the bog,
I could eat a horse,
I'd go on the teacher's course.

I could be a crab,
I could sit on a slab,
I could be called Woffie,
I'd hide under your coffee.

I could count to three,
I could buzz like a bee,
I could go to so many places,
I'd wear braces.

I could,
I could,
I could do so many things,
I'd go and eat Cheestrings,
Yes, yes I could.

Samuel Hayes (10)
Parish Church Junior School, Croydon

The Willow Tree

Down in the woods there's a willow tree at night
Where the brave campers hike.
They go through the woods,
With no sort of hoods,
But the willow tree gives them a fright!

Savannah Simmons (9)
Parish Church Junior School, Croydon

The Volcano

I'm the most vicious creature in this land,
What could I possibly be?
Exiling so many people at once,
With one single sneeze!

I'm always hungry, my stomach rumbling,
My blood is red and thick.
With my oozing, bubbling, red-orange blood,
You cannot take the mick.

I sneeze when I feel like it,
I'm the boss of me!
For when I sneeze my terrible sneeze,
Surely the people must flee.

If they do not flee quickly enough,
They'll drown in my blood - not!
Instead they'll scorch in my lava-blood,
I've shown them what I've got!

If that plan fails (I don't think so!)
I've got more up my sleeve,
I'll release my toxic gases, phew!
Then surely they must leave.

Nana Addo-Kufuor (11)
Parish Church Junior School, Croydon

Happiness

Happiness is blue like the bright blue sky,
It tastes like strawberries and cream,
It smells hot and sweet,
It looks like a bowl of chocolates,
It sounds like a saxophone playing jazz,
It feels like an enormous splash.

Beatrix McCrae (8)
Parish Church Junior School, Croydon

Inside My Magic Box
(Based on 'Magic Box' by Kit Wright)

I will put in my box . . .
An ancient spatula from the Stone Age,
The boiled water from a saucepan,
The world's best strand of spaghetti.

I will put in my box . . .
The fresh meat from a pig,
God's all-so-powerful hands,
The mince from a lamb.

I will put in my box . . .
The picked thyme at three o'clock,
The tomato sauce from the world's biggest tomato.

I will make my box from
The material of Jamie Oliver's hat
And the hinges from the dough of a hot dog.

I want to become in my box . . .
A cheque in my box,
I want to see the finest grape,
I want to see the biggest tomato,
And I want to see the world.

Joshua Bastock (10)
Parish Church Junior School, Croydon

Sadness

Sadness is blue and white like the clouds covering the blue sky,
It tastes like sour blueberries running in the cold,
It smells like light smoke curling in the sky,
It looks like white smoke twisting in a spiral,
It sounds like people weeping in the darkness,
It feels like a big invisible ball trapping you inside.

Ella Smoker (8)
Parish Church Junior School, Croydon

When I'm Older I Will

I will, I will,
I will run the marathon,
I will buy a horse,
I will eat a snail,
I will do no chores.

I will be on TV,
I will have a baby,
I will buy a mansion,
I will be famous, just maybe.

I will get a husband,
I will get a lovely car,
I will run my own business,
I will have my own juice bar.

I will go to Hawaii,
I will write a book,
I will invent something amazing,
I will learn how to cook.

I will do all this,
Just if my mummy lets me!

Ella Dunn (10)
Parish Church Junior School, Croydon

Candy!

C andy tastes so good
A ll sorts of candy
N ice and scrummy candy to eat, all for me
D elicious candy, sticky, big, small
Y ummy candy, all sorts of candy, *just for me!*

Yummy candy in my belly,
Candy tastes so good, all for me!

Deja Hutchison (10)
Parish Church Junior School, Croydon

The Magic Box
(Based on 'Magic Box' by Kit Wright)

I will put in my box . . .
The everlasting tail of a Chinese dragon,
The igniting feathers of a phoenix, flickering light,
A winged lion who is proud and mighty.

I will put in my box . . .
Silk of a chestnut shell in autumn,
The summer breeze,
The fragrance of the flowers of spring,
A pinch of snow from winter.

I will put in my box . . .
My first sight of the outside,
The last breath of my grandparents,
The last day and the last life.

I will put in my box . . .
The light of life,
The darkness of death.

I will think in my box
About the past, present and future.

Michael Mensah (11)
Parish Church Junior School, Croydon

Riddles

You wear me on your ears
And I help you see,
Without me you can't see.
I come in many colours
And shapes and sizes.
What am I?

A: Glasses.

Bonita Fearon (9)
Parish Church Junior School, Croydon

My River Song

The river's long,
Plus it loves to sing a song.
It goes on and on.

Its song is so calm,
You can doze off when you're near it.
Year in, year out, except for one season,
Of course that's winter.

It's calm, quiet and peaceful,
Of course that's great too,
But then summer always comes round again.

Then it gets louder,
But sweeter by the minute.
Now the splash is coming,
I'm ready to fall, fall, fall in it.

Now it is free, running into the sea,
It still goes on, singing the same old song,
Forever, for you and for me.

Benjamin Fifield (10)
Parish Church Junior School, Croydon

Happiness

Happiness is like the colour of the bright golden sun,
It tastes like the yummiest ice cream ever!
It smells like a bunch of fresh lavender on a summer's day,
It sounds like the birds chirping in the beautiful clouds
of the calm blue sky.
It looks like the bright moon and the sparkly stars
of a tranquil night,
It feels like a soft, cuddly teddy bear staring into your eyes
like an innocent little puppy.

Tariq Shakur Badshah (8)
Parish Church Junior School, Croydon

A Cloud Full Of Dreams

I look up at the sky
And I see clouds floating by,
White, fluffy, shaped like cotton wool,
High up in the sky.

Hours of sunshine,
More fun for us,
I wonder what it would be like
To stand upon a cloud.

Ladybirds and butterflies all flying by,
Take in the sunshine
And rest for a nap,
Tempting as it sounds,
I'd rather watch the world go by.

Hours of sunshine,
More fun for us,
I wonder what it would be like
To stand upon a cloud.

Laura Stoneham (9)
Parish Church Junior School, Croydon

The Building

The building stood up,
It wished it was a person.
The building asked, 'Why am I a building?
I am not a building, I am a duck.'
The building ate a banana,
The building stamped his feet and went to bed,
Changed his mind, wished he was dead.
The next morning he woke up,
Turned out he was a duck.
The duck said, 'I'm out of luck.'

Tom Brunswick (9)
Parish Church Junior School, Croydon

I Could

I could run ten miles,
I could eat an ox,
I could be a runner,
A doctor,
A duck,
A dog,
A donkey.
I could run five miles,
I could eat a zebra,
A could be a dentist,
A doctor,
A duck,
A dog,
A donkey,
Or I could watch TV,
Or eat a chicken nugget,
Or be a weather lady,
Or go to bed, so goodnight!

Amber Atouguia (10)
Parish Church Junior School, Croydon

Love

Love is kind,
Love is considerate,
Love is like a sunset of different colours.
The bible says,
Love always trusts, hopes and protects,
Love is like fizzy popping candy on your tongue,
Love sounds like beautiful harps,
Love is when you give your brother your last sweet
and you didn't want to,
Love is for everyone.

Liah Danquah (8)
Parish Church Junior School, Croydon

The Night Of Fright

One day I woke up and saw
My parents had left a note by my door.
I picked it up to see what they wrote,
Then I looked at the door to see their coats.
Their coats weren't there on the door,
So I tripped over and had a great fall!

My parents had gone out of town, you see,
So it was just my hamster and me.
I was really bored and really sad
Although I was a tiny bit glad
Because the *whole* house was for me and my hamster!

Then at night I went to bed
And I heard someone say, 'Get up, bed-head!'
I pulled the duvet right over my head.
'Get up you!' the mean person said.
I didn't know what to do, I didn't know what to say,
I felt like screaming and peeking out of my duvet.

Hana Shafieyfard (10)
Parish Church Junior School, Croydon

Fires

Don't play with fire,
Don't play with fire,
Don't touch it,
Don't eat it,
Don't lick it
Or kick fire.

Fire, fire is a dangerous thing,
Don't hit it
Or lick it,
Or you'll be burned to a crisp.

James Moore (10)
Parish Church Junior School, Croydon

The Space Traveller

A traveller travelling through space and time,
Looking sad and lonely without any friends,
His wisdom, the only hope to achieve his dream,
To explore new worlds, not just following trends.

One day he wasn't having any luck,
Until an alien planet he came across.
A greeny-blue, atmospheric colour,
With strong gales that made the spaceship toss.

From his window a deserted, barren landscape was his first sight,
Then an alien army the traveller saw,
With hideous bodies and eyes bulging,
Screaming, the aliens charged through the door.

A traveller travelling through space and time,
Looking sad and lonely without a friend,
His wisdom the only hope to achieve his dream,
To explore new worlds, not just following trends.

Deepesh Rajeshkumar Patel (9)
Parish Church Junior School, Croydon

I Love You

I love my caring mum,
I love my caring dad,
I love my fun-to-hang-out-with stepmum,
I love my fun, funny stepdad.

I love my kind aunties,
I love my uncles who like to play football.
I love my cousins, they're the best,
Especially Messy Jessy, Smelly Sam,
Khiaran, the fireman, and Scabby Abi,

But most of all I love God!

Faith Gomez (10)
Parish Church Junior School, Croydon

The Poor Horse

As I walk down the sunset-shiny farm,
I look at the beautiful brown horse.
Neigh, neigh, is all I can hear,
Only because the poor horse is being forced,

Being forced for not eating its dinner.
Poor horse, what can it do?
For it only stands there and gets bored,
And sometimes gets the flu.

I walk over to the poor horse,
'Did that man give you a fright?
He probably didn't mean it,
He just didn't want to see you in such a sight.

Would you like me to feed you?'
Neigh, Neigh, is all I can hear.
'If you could just eat, it would bring some cheer.
Yes! Yes! That's right, you eat up, my dear.'

Shaneace Brown (10)
Parish Church Junior School, Croydon

Love

Love is red like a heart,
It tastes like warm chocolate cake,
It smells like sweet spring flowers,
It looks like a colourful rainbow
on a summer's day after a shower of rain,
It sounds like children giggling
and enjoying their time outside.
It feels like a warm hand holding onto you
to keep you safe.

Anna Lofmark (8)
Parish Church Junior School, Croydon

The River's Journey

Racing river roaring along the splashing track,
Just like an Aston Martin DB9.
Waiting wave, blink and gone,
'Grrr!' screams the river, chasing its prey.

It dances like a ballerina in a blue dress,
It conquers the corners in a game of chess.
As it zooms at the speed of light,
Suddenly day turns to night.

The river is lava pouring and oozing
Out of a vibrating volcano.
The calm water falls off the waterfall like sweets,
Tumbling into my pic 'n' mix.

But now the river is silent,
Not like a galloping gazelle,
Nor a rampaging rhino,
But like a baby snoozing.

Joy Cummings (10)
Parish Church Junior School, Croydon

Happiness

Happiness is like rain pouring down in summer,
Happiness is like young grass shining in the radiant sunlight down below,
It is like the breeze blowing through my long, silky hair,
It reminds me of the birds singing around me.
I never feel bad because happiness surrounds me,
It fades away quickly but you will never forget it.
It is my childhood memories,
I feel calm and quiet.

Lakshana Sankar (8)
Parish Church Junior School, Croydon

Seasons

Spring is wonderful, spring is new,
Colours are everywhere, pink, purple and blue.
Spring flowers are beautiful and
Gardeners are dutiful.

Summer is hot, lots to do,
We go to the seaside, and it's my birthday too!
Outings and picnics, lots of fun,
Put on a hat out in the sun.

Golden leaves fall to the ground,
Gardeners make them into a mound.
Harvest, conkers and Guy Fawkes day,
Autumn is busy, but still time to play.

Nippy and slippy in the snow,
Crisp, cold days make your faces glow.
Dark, wet nights, soup to eat,
Christmas is coming, what a treat!

Molly Bielecki (7)
Parish Church Junior School, Croydon

The Boys

There was once a boy called Minny,
His best friend was called Jimmy,
People once said, 'Hi Minny and Jimmy.'
But on Monday all of that
Was about to change.
Jimmy said, 'Let's become bullies.'
Minny didn't like it,
So they were no longer friends.

Levi Foka (10)
Parish Church Junior School, Croydon

The Haunted House

The abandoned house lives at the end of the street,
Its spine-chilling stare will send you running on your feet,
'T S Terra Nova' it says on the board, but terror is the word,
If you go inside, which wouldn't be wise, your scream won't be heard.
Its cracked windows are closed and dead,
With a rumour that has been said,
A gang of berserk, mad arch fiends once hid there,
Without less of a care.
Now it looks like a dump,
With litter and an old bicycle pump.
I always run past in one breath,
Otherwise I could face death.
No one but I knows this.
Hear it scream, yell and hiss.
An abandoned house lives at the end of the street,
Its spine-chilling stare will send you running on your feet.

Harishon Sasikaran (11)
Parish Church Junior School, Croydon

Funny Mellow

Sometimes I sit and wonder about stuff I don't know,
Like who invented funny mellow?
Did they squeeze it?
Did they heave it?
What was it like long ago?
Did they wheeze?
Did they sneeze?
What was it like long ago?

Phoebe Russell (7)
Parish Church Junior School, Croydon

Flutter By, Butterfly

Flutter by butterfly, flutter by butterfly,
With your graceful wings.
Butterfly flutter by, butterfly flutter by,
With your colourful wings.
Butterfly flutter by, butterfly flutter by
With your graceful wings.

Flutter by butterfly, with your bright and colourful wings.
Flutter by butterfly with your bright and colourful wings.
Butterfly flutter by with your graceful wings.
Butterfly flutter by with your graceful wings.

Butterfly flutter by with your beautiful wings.
Flutter by butterfly with your bright and colourful wings.
Butterfly flutter by with your beautiful wings.

Butterfly flutter by with your athletic wings.
Flutter by butterfly with your bright and colourful wings.

Shafiq Salahudeen (10)
Parish Church Junior School, Croydon

Springtime

Spring, oh spring,
How could I compare thee?
Could it be the beautiful blooms
Or the beautiful butterflies.
How about the nature
Followed by summer,
After winter,
Too far from autumn?
Spring makes my hayfever go bad.
All there is, is three months,
That's about twelve weeks.
Bye white trees, hello green trees.

Ross Maitland-Harris (10)
Parish Church Junior School, Croydon

Six Things You Would Find In David Beckham's Bag
(Inspired by 'Ten Things Found in a Wizard's Pocket' by Ian McMillan)

You would find his lucky smelly socks,
That he wore at every match.
You would find a comb with his name in glittery silver on it,
For when he changes the style of his hair.
You would find a pair of red and gold studs
That were cleaned straight away after he wore them.
You would find a blue asthma pump
For when he's out of breath.
You would find a red mirror with an England sign on it
That he uses to see if his good looks are still there.
You would find a muddy, dirty, red football kit
That he wore to all his matches.

Sade Williams (10)
Parish Church Junior School, Croydon

Monkey

Monkey, monkey, tidy up this room,
Monkey, monkey, hurry up and get the broom,
Monkey, monkey, I'm tired of this,
You scared the mouse so get out of my house.
Monkey, monkey, look at your hair,
You're just about to meet Tony Blair.
Monkey, monkey, you need to have a bath,
Take off your scarf, you're so very daft.
Monkey, monkey, stop jumping on the
door and falling on the floor.
Monkey, monkey, you have to go, don't be slow.
Monkey, monkey, see you at noon.

Shaquil Boakye (10)
Parish Church Junior School, Croydon

If Only I Had . . .

A hummingbird to sing me a sweet lullaby,
Or an eye so strong to take in all colours at once.

If only I had a paintbrush so muscular I could paint the world,
Or a garden so fertile and vast I could plant
all the flowers of the land.

If only I had all the books for the world in one
as a reference of my adventures,
Or a butterfly so exotic that it overshadowed
even the brightest of plants.

If only I had a spaceship that would allow me
to touch the untouchable rings of Saturn,
Or a voice that would sound likewise to the angels.

If only, if only . . .

Lana Headley (11)
Parish Church Junior School, Croydon

Summer - Haikus

Sea like butterflies
People tanning on the beach
Burning hot air floats

Dolphins jump to breathe
Graceful dolphins dance and leap
Gliding through the air

Boiling, burning sun
Several light years away
Bright sun lights the sky

Blazing sun shines bright
Yellow ball on a blackboard
One million earths.

Alice Ardis (8)
Parish Church Junior School, Croydon

House Alive

The disappearing door waits as the sun approaches,
Transparent windows open their insignificant eyes.
Radiators yawn - they are tigers,
ready to snatch their prey.
Elaborate, comfy sofas snuggly cosy themselves warm
as the day begins.
Old chimneys cough up the puff of smoke
to get rid of their tonsillitis.
Alarm clocks screech for England as they wobble
and break their legs.
The shower is washing itself fresh and clean,
The walls dye their hair.
The house waits for when the clock strikes 9pm,
when it falls asleep preparing for the craziness of tomorrow.

Khadijah Hayden (11)
Parish Church Junior School, Croydon

The Best Bits Of Winter

W hite blanket enveloping the landscape
I cicles hanging from the ragged rooftops
N ights drawing longer
T insel wrapped around the Christmas tree
E ntertainment indoors is the name of the game
R udolph is coming soon, so be good

I n the house it is boiling
S now outside lays thicker than ever

C old shivers down my spine overwhelm my body
O ccupy yourself with snowball fights
O mens, stay clear, this is a time of celebration
L ots of umbrellas are in everyone's houses
   whilst the cold remains.

Joel Akaje-Macauley (9)
Parish Church Junior School, Croydon

Happiness

Happiness is being joyful for something.
Happiness is a really good thing to have.
Happiness is green like lovely, healthy grass.
Happiness is like a butterfly,
The more you chase it, the more it eludes you,
But if you turn your attention to other things
It will come and sit softly on your shoulder.
It tastes like sweet lemon on a beautiful tree.
It smells delicious.
It looks like the hot sun rising up.
It sounds like everyone cheering and . . .
It feels really good.

Ope Oso (7)
Parish Church Junior School, Croydon

Fear

One day at school
I got hit by a ball
Owned by someone tall.

They called me, 'Clem and Bem,'
They said I'm small,
I called the boy tall.

The boy asked me to race
At another place,
I said, 'No!'
The boy tried to beat me up
But his mum was there!

Elise Marston (9)
Parish Church Junior School, Croydon

Scream

Scream if you know the answer to my life,
Scream if life catches you too quick,
Horror is not a dream, it is real life.

Screams on roller coasters,
Screams of joy,
Screams of happiness
And screams for a fantastic time.

Scream if you laugh your guts out,
Even if you wet yourself.
Life is to take chances,
So scream if you love life!

Kerris Redway (10)
Parish Church Junior School, Croydon

Lots Of Bullies

Bullies always have to cheat,
Bullies, bullies are in the street.

Bullies keep on acting cool,
But bullies are nothing but a fool!

They try to act good when they're alone,
They even try to act good with their phones.

I don't understand why they've got all the muscles,
And all the little ones are conquered and rustled.

Yes, I know who bullies are, but they're not quite far
From being a lemon tart!

Jerelm Rose-Clarke (10)
Parish Church Junior School, Croydon

W Is For War

I am here to serve my time
Because again I have crossed the line,
I will never see the world through true eyes
As I live in a pool of white lies.
My trust will never be given out
For I will never be forgiven, with no doubt.
I want to see the world again
And I want my heart to mend.

Natasha Fearon (11)
Parish Church Junior School, Croydon

Friendship

Friendship is yellow or smiling faces,
It tastes like sweets for best, best friends,
It smells like custard creams,
It looks like an old lady taking her dog for a walk,
It sounds like best friends shouting and playing together
in the playground,
It feels like best friends sticking together, no matter what!

Tina Bosa Bonsu (8)
Parish Church Junior School, Croydon

Love

Love is as blue as the shimmering ocean,
It tastes as creamy as smooth milk chocolate,
It smells like fresh pancakes wafting up my nose,
It looks like the most beautiful red and orange sunset,
It sounds like laughter in the air,
It feels like a gentle kiss upon my cheek.
This is what love means to me.

Megan Elliott (8)
Parish Church Junior School, Croydon

Really Cross!

Really cross is the red bit of Spider-Man's suit,
Tastes of radishes,
Smells like feet - disgusting!
Cross looks like someone crying,
Cross sounds like people making silly noises,
Cross makes me feel like lying on the floor and kicking.
Homework makes me cross!

Libby Norton (8)
Parish Church Junior School, Croydon

Spreading Circles

A pebble was just dropped in the water.
Ping, drip, drop, ripple,
Spreading circles getting bigger,
Spreading circles getting bigger,
Hot day,
Steamy evaporation,
The pool is still and smooth.

Samuel Oliver-Rowland (10)
Parish Church Junior School, Croydon

Melancholy

Melancholy is blue like the midnight seas of February,
It's the tang of bitter seawater on your lips,
It smells like the embers of a dying fire,
It looks like a lonely child in a playground,
It sounds like the weak hoot of a distant owl,
It feels like a shiver around your waist!

Leah Terry (8)
Parish Church Junior School, Croydon

All About Love!

Love is as red as a rose,
Tastes like strawberries on a summer day,
Smells so lush and sweet,
Looks like a field of roses,
Sounds of laughter,
Feels like a great big hug.

Lauren Hawkes (7)
Parish Church Junior School, Croydon

Love

Love is red like a bunch of roses,
Love tastes like a creamy, hot dessert on a wintery day,
Love smells like a fountain of runny chocolate,
Love looks like two red cheeks,
Love sounds like a sweet violin tune,
Love feels like the greatest gift of all.

Thomas Smolen (8)
Parish Church Junior School, Croydon

Happiness

Happiness is like the radiant sun,
Beating down on you on a summer's day.
Happiness is something people can never take away.
Happiness tastes like strawberries,
Cream and ice cream on a Friday night.
Happiness smells like bacon sizzling in a frying pan.

Emma Grummitt (8)
Parish Church Junior School, Croydon

Love

Love is as red as a red, red rose,
It tastes like a red berry on a tree,
It smells like ripe cherries,
It looks like fireworks booming in the air,
It sounds like angels singing on the clouds,
It feels like Heaven!

Dénae Chung (8)
Parish Church Junior School, Croydon

Happiness

It smells like the deep sea breeze,
It tastes like a scrumptious ice cream,
It looks like a bunch of roses,
It sounds like a wave coming to the bright yellow sand,
It feels like running your hand along a field of daisies,
It is as bright as the sun on a summer's day.

Ryan Crockett (7)
Parish Church Junior School, Croydon

Love

Love is red like a deep, dark red rose,
It tastes like strawberries and cream with lots of sugar,
It smells like the sweet smell of flowers,
It looks like crystals sparkling in the moonlight,
It sounds like a sparkle of magic from the fairy godmother's wand,
It feels like the warmth of the sun beating down on you.

Ellie-Dawn Wenham (8)
Parish Church Junior School, Croydon

Calmness

Calmness is light blue like the bright morning sky,
It tastes like lovely fresh fruit,
It smells like a beautiful rose,
It looks like a calm beach,
It sounds like the calm waves of an ocean,
It feels like a warm, comfy bed!

Edwina Ansong (8)
Parish Church Junior School, Croydon

Tiger, Tiger

Tiger, tiger sleeping in the sauna,
Tiger, tiger creeping round the corner.
Tiger, tiger reading The Times,
Tiger, tiger eating lemon and lime.
Tiger, tiger prepares to have lunch,
Tiger, tiger, so you'd better run!

Natalie Ayim-Owusu (11)
Parish Church Junior School, Croydon

Dancing

Dancing is my way of life,
It makes me feel alive.
The music beats to my feet,
Tap my feet.

Ayanna Korsah (9)
Parish Church Junior School, Croydon

War

I'm as old as time and life
Which is more than you would ever imagine.

I'm the darkest colour
You will ever see
In your whole life.

I taste like burned fire
From the past.

I smell like ash,
Ash from red, steaming fire.

I live on the hard,
Dirty, rough ground.

I kill and
Make sorrow for others.

I'm afraid of nothing,
Nothing can hurt me.

Katherine Zuleta Gil (9)
Riverside Primary School, London

I Make The World Go Round

I'm older than all living and not living things put together.
I sit in everyone's heart then grow with love,
And it doesn't take long because love is everywhere.
I make the world go round with love
And make the world a lovable place.
I fear sorrow and woe because that will make
Cupid's arrows shine with love no longer.
I am proud of my work -
I put love in and banish hatred.
I am friendship.

Ryan Lieu (10)
Riverside Primary School, London

The Wonderful Soul

I am as old as the gazing stars
Which gleam and fill your soul with joy.
I live deep in the heart, growing every day
And creating a beautiful relationship.
I put broken loyalties together and
Extend trust for the future
So it can be shared with others.
I am afraid of deceiving and those who lie
To gain a trust which they want to destroy
Because of what they have gone through.
I am proud of everlasting love
Which many people produce for who they are.
The wonderful soul of people
Which shines like the sun.
Their love never runs out because of my caring.
I am friendship.

Francis Kanneh (11)
Riverside Primary School, London

Older Than The Human Race

I am as old as the first creatures who met on Earth,
Even older than the human race.
I live deep down beneath everyone's heart
And I always will, even if you don't know it.
I fix the smile on your face
By sending you someone to share and have fun with.
I am afraid of hate as it breaks me in half.
I am proud of the way I join souls together,
And of all the good I do for the world.
The sun represents me as it is always there,
Even if you can't see it.
I am friendship.

Alma Crasmaru (11)
Riverside Primary School, London

Love And Courage

Courage smells like bravery,
Courage sounds like a strong person that believes in themselves,
Courage feels like a good feeling inside your body,
Courage looks like a person that has faith in themselves,
Courage tastes like a sweet taste running through your mouth,
Courage is the colour blue,
Courage is tall like a mountain,
Courage is small like a button,
Courage moves like a dog,
Courage is quiet as a mouse.
Love smells like perfume,
Love sounds like a love song being played in the midnight sky,
Love feels like a gentle touch on your skin,
Love looks like a rose in the lovely green fields,
Love tastes like chocolate melting in your mouth.

Daniela Monteiro (10)
Riverside Primary School, London

Spreading Peace

I am as old as old can get
And no one knows where I create and give my gift.
I live in the heart of everything and I cannot be shattered.
I produce life and happiness which keeps me going.
I am afraid of jealousy which reduces me to tears,
Which burns my heart away.
I am proud of keeping people together,
Even when they are apart.
Just like the sun in the sky, it is always there,
Even when it is not visible.
I am like a white dove sweeping through the sky
Spreading happiness and peace.
I am friendship.

Kitty Widdows (10)
Riverside Primary School, London

Love

Love smells like happiness
And a love strike just hit you.
Love sounds like a dark night on a beach
And a full moon listening to the waves.
Love feels like a dream
And it feels like Valentine's Day
Repeating itself very day.
Love looks like Valentines and your happy heart.
Love tastes like sweet candy.
Love's colour is like a rainbow and
An Earth of lovely rainbow colours.
Love is tall like the world,
Love is small like Pluto, the smallest planet.
Love is warm like the sun in Hawaii,
Love is cold like an igloo in Antarctica.

Georgie Howell (10)
Riverside Primary School, London

Bravery

Bravery smells like the tasty smell of bush meat,
Bravery sounds like the triumphant calling of a brave warrior,
Bravery feels like the crowd cheering for you
out of your brave deeds,
Bravery looks like a golden chalice waiting to be
given to a courageous man,
Bravery tastes like freshly picked berries with a juicy centre,
The colour of bravery is fiery red with misty orange
in the background,
Bravery has its length which leads to Heaven,
Bravery grows with the help of courage.

Blessing Aroboto (10)
Riverside Primary School, London

I Live In The Soul

I am infinity years old,
I am older than the Earth,
I am older than a heart.
I live in the soul, deep, deep down.
I live on flowers,
I live in the sea that washes the land.
I bring people together day and night,
I spread love around.
I am afraid that my heart will burn from sadness.
I am proud of making everyone happy.
I am friendship.

Lisa Bushby (10)
Riverside Primary School, London

Aggression Grows

Aggression grows very, very fast,
It feels like the hot sun has just rushed into my heart.
Aggression sounds like three bass guitars breaking their strings,
It looks like a ball that's very, very thick.
Aggression tastes like a mind controller and you can't get out.
Aggression is very tall and no one can get taller than it, no doubt.
Aggression is grey and you can't change the colour.
Aggression is not small and the more tall,
the more horrible the surprises.
It moves its legs and it does it every day,
And that's all I have to say.

Anita Milton-Hunter (10)
Riverside Primary School, London

Afraid Of A Teardrop

I am as old as gods and angels in Heaven,
Up above in the heavenly sky.
I live in the heart and soul
Of every breathing creature on planet Earth.
I go around to find new relationships
And make people happy and proud of themselves.
I am afraid of a teardrop from someone's eye
And a broken heart full of hate.
I am proud of creating happiness and joy
In people's hearts.
I am friendship.

Ibraheem Keshinro (10)
Riverside Primary School, London

Afraid Of Nothing

I am as old as the Earth and will stay
For eternity with the gods in the heavens.
I live in the hearts of every person
And every living creature.
I put together friends and try
To banish hatred from every soul.
I am afraid of nothing because my gift
Can banish jealousy and bad feelings.
I am proud of all everlasting friends.
I am friendship.

Zayn Ali (10)
Riverside Primary School, London

In People's Hearts And Minds

I am as old as the Earth itself
And the gods above.
I live in people's hearts and minds.
I combine hearts together
To make people happy.
I am afraid of people's hatred
And their dark side.
I am proud of making
People's hearts feel good.
I am friendship!

Ryan Sexton (11)
Riverside Primary School, London

I Live In The Heart

I am as old as the gods in the heavens above,
I live in the heart, mind and soul of the universe.
I reach for the troubled souls
And give them love, joy and passion.
I am afraid of the darkness lurking within time and space,
Seeking to annihilate happiness.
I am proud of the gift I have given to the world.
I am giving you my gift to enable you
To reach within yourself and release your kindness.
I am friendship.

Ibrahim Doumbia (11)
Riverside Primary School, London

Surprise

Surprise smells like a random object,
Surprise sounds like a soul being squished,
Surprised feels like a box with a wrapper,
Surprise looks like a big black box,
Surprise tastes like a bag of sweets,
Surprise's colour is like a portal to another dimension,
Surprise is as tall as a giraffe on stilts,
Surprise is as small as a drop of mouse blood,
Surprise creeps up on people, infecting them with surprise,
Surprise continuously grows until it's revealed.

Alexander Melnikov (10)
Riverside Primary School, London

The Horror Of Fear

I am as old as the Earth.
I represent darkness, the grey clouds clashed together.
I taste like dry blood from a man that has been killed.
I smell like a gun that has just been fired.
I live in a field far away where houses are crushed
And turned into other things,
While parents are crying for their houses.
I am thrown around and then I explode and kill people.
I fear nothing because I am like a god.

Blessing Kingston (9)
Riverside Primary School, London

Never-Ending Circle

I am as old as time itself in a never-ending circle.
I live in everything you see and in hearts of joy.
I travel through time
Seeking those in need.
I'm afraid of blood dripping from a human's heart
Filled with sorrow and hatred.
I am proud of my seed which is growing in hearts.
I am friendship.

Damilula Odumusi (11)
Riverside Primary School, London

War

I am as old as time,
I am the colour of people's blood,
from the people on the battlefield.
I taste like blood from dead people,
I smell like poison, from the dark stew.
I live in the dark grey sky, where the cities get bombed.
I am the reason war starts,
I am afraid of nothing.

Megan Lynch (9)
Riverside Primary School, London

Wonder Forever

Wonder smells like a field of daffodils,
Wonder sounds like a choir of birds singing,
Wonder feels like a little silky puppy,
Wonder looks like a room full of lots and lots of pictures,
Wonder tastes like sweet and luxury,
Wonder is blue and white all over.

Mercedese Roach (10)
Riverside Primary School, London

War

I don't have an age,
I have existed forever and will exist for evermore.
I am the colour of war (green and brown like the battlefields).
I taste like burn metal that has been hit with fire,
I smell like a fireball that has just exploded.
I live in the fields of war in Bermondsey.
I shoot bombs onto the target and kill them.
I am afraid of nothing in the world.

Rachael Fagbodun (9)
Riverside Primary School, London

Love

Love smells like roses,
Love sounds like a kiss,
It feels like Liverpool,
It tastes like lemon lips.
Its colour is pink.
Tall it is.
It moves like kissing.
It grows like a firework.

Alfie Butler (10)
Riverside Primary School, London

Courage

Courage smells like a sweet smell that won't give up.
Courage tastes like a sweet but bitter dream.
Courage is a colour of its own, no one can describe it.
Courage can be as small as a mouse when it's lost,
But courage grows as fast as a train when you find it.

Sophia Wahidullah (10)
Riverside Primary School, London

War

I am 900 years old like the trees that get blown down.
I am the colour of the grey smoke that floats in the air.
I taste like metal equipment.
I smell like smoke from a bomb after it drops.
I live in cold, dark, fabric tents.
I work in the war fighting for destiny.
I am not afraid of anything.

Kheira Stambouli (9)
Riverside Primary School, London

War

I am 49 and I live on my own.
My colour is burnt, old, muddy skin.
I smell like old muddy feet.
I live in a dirty shed.
I shoot people for a living.
I am afraid of people shooting me.
I taste like dirty feet which have been crawling in mud.

Kacie Ervin (9)
Riverside Primary School, London

War

I'm 18 years old but I look like nine,
I'm the colour of golden bullets shooting at me,
I taste like grenade smoke,
I smell like dead bodies,
I live in a tunnel with the rest of the army,
I killed Hitler and the Nazis,
I am not afraid of anything.

Harry Bradley (9)
Riverside Primary School, London

I Wonder

I wonder what it would be like
To never be seen,
I wonder what it would be like
To be as small as a baked bean.

I wonder what it would be like
To have a million feet,
I wonder what it would be like
If people never had to eat.

I wonder what it would be like
To be in the middle of the sea,
I wonder what it would be like
If everyone looked up to me.

I wonder what it would be like
If we were in the Ice Age,
I wonder what it would be like
To jump into a book's page.

I wonder what it would be like
To ride a griffin,
I wonder what it would be like
To run a race and win.

I wonder what it would be like
To meet the Queen,
I wonder what it would be like
To be very, very mean.

Jaimie Osborne (9)
St John's CE Primary School, Wellington

Sports Day

I see the other members running
Full speed, straight past me,
So I had to speed up my pace super-fast.

I heard my team cheering very loud,
So I had to run like the wind,
I couldn't let my team down.

But then suddenly I fell to the ground,
While I shut my eyes, thinking it's all a dream,
But then I fell to the ground and then
I know it's not a dream.

While I'm on the ground
I hold onto the grass tightly,
But then I open my eyes
And see that I'm first.

Because as I fall, I zoom over the finish line,
But before I get my trophy,
I get a compliment on my smelly armpits.

Megan Blest (10)
St John's CE Primary School, Wellington

My Horse

Her sleek, black body like the starry night sky,
The shiny, gleaming coat dazzles in the warm sunshine,
Her long tail swoops silently in the light breeze.
Gracefully her hooves trot very slowly,
With leaves swirling around them.
The magnificent mane flies around
As the strong wind tugs at it.
Curiously her soft eyes stare at me
Like emerald-green ivy leaves.

Ellys Webb (7)
St John's CE Primary School, Wellington

The Sea

In the sea there are beautiful fish
Swimming happily
With coral and clams and other creatures
That live in the oceans.

In the sea there are mighty sharks
Trying to find some fish to eat,
But dolphins scare them away,
To not eat multicoloured fish.

In the sea there are clownfish
With orange and white stripes,
And swordfishes with long, sharp noses,
Which they can fight with.

In the sea there are the fishes fast asleep,
Waiting for another day
To swim about and play about,
Until that day has gone too.

Kian Stafford (10)
St John's CE Primary School, Wellington

Ice Cream

I love tall ice creams because
There's more to eat.
Dizzy, delicious ice cream staring at me,
Waiting to be eaten.
Rumbling, hungry tummies waiting
For the cold, dripping ice cream,
Nice, icy cold, delicious sauce dripping down
Dazzling ice cream,
Our mouths watering like a running tap,
Sprinkles, all colourful, shaken on top,
Finished with a cherry on top.

Madison Davey (8)
St John's CE Primary School, Wellington

Chrysanthemum

Filled with a fresh personality and smell
Which whiffs of Heaven,
The flower is a delight.
Soft petals that vary in size,
As delicate as a single feather.
Their petals are daisy-like,
Layering over each other and
Crowding around its pollen.
The flowers range in colour
From a bright cerise and peach
To fuchsia, lavender and white.
Its stem is a delightful verdant stem
That stands proud and never slouches.
The flower looks completely stunning
With droplets of clear water
Sparkling on each petal.

Shannon Nutkins (10)
St John's CE Primary School, Wellington

My Dream

I can see the sun shining in my eyes
And hitting me in the mouth,
And at night, the glistening stars.
I can smell fresh milk chocolate
And some candy and the
Chocolate saying, 'Please eat me.'
It feels like I am on Candyland and
Candy sticks to your bare feet.
I feel marshmallows zooming past my face.
I am catching a bunch of chewy, chewy gummy bears,
But when I catch them I squash them
With my shoes by accident.

Jaime-Leigh Napper (9)
St John's CE Primary School, Wellington

Snow Leopard

The snow leopard's paws are killer paws,
Stomping through the snow.

It's long, bendy tail swishes through the air
As the leopard walks along.

Strong legs for walking great distances
And for killing its prey.

Its patterned body rumbles in the night,
Waiting for the leopard to hunt.

Twitching ears, listening out for danger,
Golden, glaring eyes fixed on its prey.

Lauren Thorne (11)
St John's CE Primary School, Wellington

Axolotl

Tender, slim threadlike legs
To float out into the wide open sea.
Cute, button-like eyes to search
For its vicious prey.
Spiky antennae which appear like pointed spears.
A tiny, unnoticeable line as a mouth
For blowing bubbles within the ocean.
A sharp point as a tail
That vibrates to make it travel.
A small body that roams the midnight ocean
Whilst the other sea animals are asleep.

Sharnie Jenkins (11)
St John's CE Primary School, Wellington

Romans Vs Celts

Romans, as scary as thunder crashes,
Adventurous armies approach,
Angry Celts attack!
Dangerous Celts fight as the Romans battle,
Fierce Celts battle bravely
But the Romans conquer Britannia.
The Celts' spears glide through the air
Like a cannonball.
The Romans invaded Britannia.
Romans and Celts.

Benjamin Williams (8)
St John's CE Primary School, Wellington

Star Wars

Quickly the Jedi pull out their lightsabers
To kill their enemies,
To win the battle.
Lightsabers are blue, green, red and purple.
General Grevious, with four hands and lightsabers,
A brilliant fighter.
Shooting around space in their spaceship,
Destroying the enemy.

Robin Provis (8)
St John's CE Primary School, Wellington

My Dog

My dog is a good dog, he's funny.
I take my dog for a walk around the park.
He runs and jumps
Then he licks his bone.

Simon Hollis (9)
St John's CE Primary School, Wellington

Beautiful Sunsets

Sunsets beautifully settling down for night-time,
Pretty, colourful, just like summer.
Sparkling, gorgeous sun glistens on the ocean,
Looking like glitter.
It is bright and gorgeous,
Just like the pretty colours of a rainbow.
Wonderful, sparkling, just like snow.
Beautiful sunsets.

Bethany Jade Fox (8)
St John's CE Primary School, Wellington

Fairy

Glittery wings for flying great distances,
Mini body that glows at night,
Wand that you can see far away,
Tiny feet for not making a sound,
Sparkly diamonds around their necks,
Blonde hair like a sun,
Luminous green dresses
For being seen in the moonlit sky.

Andrew Hollis & Tyler Wilkinson (11)
St John's CE Primary School, Wellington

Water

Water, nice and clear like ice melting.
Water splashing us,
Cooling us down.
In winter it's like diamonds
And sparkles like jewels.
Rain falls like tears from Heaven.

Leah Osborne (7)
St John's CE Primary School, Wellington

Dragons

The strong, powerful dragon flung his tail around.
The massive, breathing dragon blowing fire everywhere.
A huge, massive dragon showed his sharp white teeth.
A big dragon scared a young knight.
One night a huge dragon flew through the dark, cloudy sky.
A huge, scary dragon jumped up and down.
On a fire lava cliff, someone jumped up and broke a massive tooth.
A big dragon flew through the sky.

James Eva (7)
St John's CE Primary School, Wellington

Football

Happy people cheering at the match.
I score a fantastic goal,
Excited people start to shout,
'Hooray! Hooray!'
The referee blows the whistle.
The winning team collect the cup,
Everyone is happy.

Connor Cole (8)
St John's CE Primary School, Wellington

Dolphins

The intelligent dolphin swimming all over the beautiful ocean.
Dolphins playfully jump about in the dazzling water.
Gleaming, graceful dolphins twirling in the water
Like leaves falling from a tree.
Her friendly smile grins at me like a picture in the sand.
My noisy dolphin jumps about cheekily
From the water into the air.

Megan White (8)
St John's CE Primary School, Wellington

Tigers

Bright, golden eyes watching out for its next meal,
Soft, peach nose sniffing for danger,
Striped, fluffy ears listening for prey,
Small mouth ready for a snack,
Long, delicate whiskers that snap like twigs,
Solid, sturdy legs, ready for a chase.

Sophie Ward (11)
St John's CE Primary School, Wellington

Ice Cream

Cold ice cream waiting to be eaten quickly.
Chocolatey sauce waiting on the counter.
Lots of different flavours of ice cream sold in an ice cream shop.
Minty ice cream, cool and ready for the summer.
Crunchy cones holding the ice cream up.
I love yummy ice cream.

Evie Knight (7)
St John's CE Primary School, Wellington

The Tigers

The cute tigers glared at me,
The fierce growl scared me away.
The quick tiger ran across the land.
The beautiful tiger stared at my eyes.
The hairy tigers looked like fluffy balls.

Reece Webber (8)
St John's CE Primary School, Wellington

Robin Hood

Bravely Robin Hood used a crossbow to fight,
The nasty sheriff hunts him down.
Robin and his merry men had a big fight,
They hid in the woods like frightened deer
Then pounced on their enemies like angry lions.

Jack Mason (7)
St John's CE Primary School, Wellington

Seashells

The shiny shells on the yellow, stony sand,
Flat shells on the bottom of the calm sea,
The shells floating in the blue, bright sea,
All shapes and sizes.

Amy Thorne (7)
St John's CE Primary School, Wellington

Seas

Waves yellow,
Waves red,
Waves green,
Waves blue,
Waves colossal and small.

Seaweed sloppy,
Seaweed thin,
Seaweed green,
Seaweed slimy.

Fish, fins,
Fish slimy,
Fish rainbow,
Fish fat and thin.

Billy Millar (8)
St Peter's CE (VC) Junior School, Marlborough

Monsters!

Monsters fat,
Monsters scary,
Monsters thin
And monsters hairy.
Monsters colossal,
Monsters titchy,
Monsters colourful
And monsters itchy.
Monsters red,
Monsters blue,
Monsters green
And yellow too.
Monsters' fur thick,
Monsters' fur thin,
Monsters' fur soft
And also like a tin.
Monsters happy,
Monsters sad,
Monsters angry
And monsters mad!

And . . . *bang!*
The monsters all collide.
Boom!

Rohan Ball (9)
St Peter's CE (VC) Junior School, Marlborough

Happiness

Happiness smells like
A hot apple pie
With a scoop of ice cream
On a hot, sunny day.

Happiness is
Pink,
Yellow,
Orange too!

Happiness makes me feel
Like I am in a world
Of beautiful flowers.

Happiness reminds me
Of an orchard
Full of bright colours
And all the animals
Coming to greet me
And my friends.

Happiness looks like
The sun with
All the sun rays
Lending out a helping hand.

Harriet Thatcher (11)
St Peter's CE (VC) Junior School, Marlborough

Silence

Silence tastes
Like an unknown
Decision.

        Silence is as white
        As a cloud
        In the sky.

Silence sounds like
One grain of sand
Hitting a stone.

        Silence feels
        Like air
        Coming to life.

Silence looks like
A person
Thinking.

        Silence reminds
        Us of really hard
        School work.

Silence!

Michael De Val (11)
St Peter's CE (VC) Junior School, Marlborough

Dogs

Dogs bark like this
Woof!
Dogs beg and bark
Dogs run and walk
Dogs bark like this
Woof!
Dogs roll over
Dogs bite and sleep
Zzzzzzzzzzz
Dogs bark like this
Woof!
Dogs jump and lie down
Good boy, James
Dogs bark like this
Woof!
Dogs chase and lick
Dogs chew and chew
Dogs bark like this
Woof!
Dogs are my best friends.

Joseph Fillis (8)
St Peter's CE (VC) Junior School, Marlborough

At The Fair

The sweets are as soft as a cloud and as
Hard as a rock, but people
Enjoy them a lot.

Fun, fun, fun it is at the fair
Apples are nice coated in honey
Ice creams are yummy in my tummy
Roller coasters are fun and scary.

Oesa Astley (7)
St Peter's CE (VC) Junior School, Marlborough

Summer

Summer is fun
Summer is bright
Summer is all around
Summer is vacation time as well
Flowers grow
Just like you and me

On the beach speedboats
Dive into the salty sea
With great speed, off they go
Wheeeeee is all we on the beach can hear
From the very noisy people on the small boat
But all of a sudden . . .
Surf's up!

The waves go crazy,
The beach sand is basically deserted
But the sea has more friends than ever.
Anyway, it's time for me to go,
So ta-ta for now!

Zoe Hammond (9)
St Peter's CE (VC) Junior School, Marlborough

Love

Love feels like a warm summer breeze
Slowly falling down onto me
With birds singing like angels

Love looks like a gorgeous pink sunset
And love tastes like strawberries
Mixed with sugar

Love is like an angel singing and dancing
In a bunch of multicoloured flowers.

Emily Heard (11)
St Peter's CE (VC) Junior School, Marlborough

Anger

The anger rises,
The red mist descends.
You know nobody,
You have no friends.
The feral in you has just stirred,
The people around you are unnerved.
You feel like a dragon with sharp teeth and claws,
You want to crush their skulls with your massive jaws.
No one's innocent, they're all just bad,
You're not sane, you've gone mad.
The teacher's coming. You don't care.
If she tells you off it won't be fair.
They're holding you down, pressing you to the floor,
Suddenly you don't feel angry anymore.
The mist is fading, you're feeling numb,
The combat's over and the fighting's done.
Your parents will be told after school,
But you won't cry because crying's not cool.

Thomas Padfield (11)
St Peter's CE (VC) Junior School, Marlborough

Wonder

The colour of wonder is blue,
as blue as an atmospheric sky.
The sight of wonder is a sun never setting
on the dullest day.
The taste of wonder is salty
like the bottom of the sea.
The smell of wonder is baking chocolate cake
as creamy as a cloud.
The sound of wonder is a buzzing
of the oven scorching food.

Mathew Hogg (11)
St Peter's CE (VC) Junior School, Marlborough

Summer

Summer is warm
Summer is bright
Summer is everywhere
And will never go.

Flowers grow just like you
Flowers fall from blossom trees.

Summer is warm
Summer is bright
Summer is everywhere
And will never go.

On the shore the boat goes *vroom*
Like a wave in the sky.

Summer is warm
Summer is bright
Summer is as yellow as a banana!
Ah, banana!

India Bloomfield (8)
St Peter's CE (VC) Junior School, Marlborough

Winter

Snow is soft and fluffy,
But it is cold so wear your hat and gloves.
On the road it's very slippy,
So make sure your tyres are very grippy.
At Christmas the bells go *ding-ding*,
And at the end of the day they go *jing-a-ling-a-ling*.
Make a set of snowballs, throw them at my brother,
When one of them comes at you - *take cover!*
Make a big ball of snow and *splodge*,
It crashes on the window.

Ethan Payne (9)
St Peter's CE (VC) Junior School, Marlborough

Wasps

Wasps, wasps
Buzz, buzz.
Wasps, wasps
Sting, sting.

Here comes the queen wasp
Stinging everybody.
Here comes the queen wasp
Telling everybody.

Wasps are big
Wasps are small
Watch out
They're giving their all.

Wasps, wasps
Buzz, buzz.
Wasps, wasps
Sting, sting.

Aaron O'Connell (8)
St Peter's CE (VC) Junior School, Marlborough

Pain

Pain as purple as your veins
Sometimes a sharp pinch or
Other times a piercing pain
Pain sounds like hearts cracking
And people screaming
When they're being tortured
Pain tastes like a sour satsuma
Pain looks like a mammoth-sized needle
Ready to strike at any moment
It reminds me of when
I badly hurt myself skateboarding.

Harvey Millar (11)
St Peter's CE (VC) Junior School, Marlborough

Singing

Sing loud
Sing soft
Sing proud
Sing like a sloth
Meh, meh, meh, meh, meh
Lah, lah, lah, lah, lah
Sing small
Sing big
Sing tall
Sing while doing a jig
Doh, doh, doh, doh, doh
Rah, rah, rah, rah, rah
Sing with a tear
Sing with a cheer
Sing with a smile
Sing forever.

Talia Lovell-Clelford (9)
St Peter's CE (VC) Junior School, Marlborough

Love

Love is the sound of tweeting birds in the bushes.
Love is a gorgeous pink shimmering in the sunlight.
Love feels like the world is opening to everyone as the
summer breeze blows through my hair.
Love tastes of the sensation of oozing chocolate spreading
in my mouth and throat.
Love looks like a rosy diamond under the sun's bright rays.
Love reminds me of the summer nights
when I am with my family and friends.
It also reminds me of the feelings I have when I am with
the most important people in my life.

Becky Slade (11)
St Peter's CE (VC) Junior School, Marlborough

The South & South West

Courage

Courage sounds like a soldier's brave heart
Beating slowly to match his march.
Its colour is dark orange,
Like the setting sun on a scorching evening.
Courage feels brave and strong, always willing to do a task,
Always completing it.
The tasty sensation is warm and joyful,
Giving you bursts of energy when freedom is in sight.
Courage looks like a brave knight on a horse
With his lance equipped and charging,
Destroying and obliterating the task at hand.
It smells like the sweat of a thousand soldiers
Dying for their country.
It reminds me of the soldiers at war, dying
With their courageous battle cries hanging in their throats.

Andrew Boothman (11)
St Peter's CE (VC) Junior School, Marlborough

Dizzy Bees

Bees *buzz, buzz*
Bees *zzzz, zzzz*
Bees are busy by big bears
Pulling pollen out of pansies

Bees *buzz, buzz*
Bees *zzzz, zzzz*
Bees stinging people
Looking for flowers

Bees *buzz, buzz*
Bees *buzz, buzz*
Like a wasp having a fight
Making honey in a hive.

Dylan Barnes (7)
St Peter's CE (VC) Junior School, Marlborough

Rallying Cars
(In memory of Colin McRae)

We
Now
Present
Marvellous Colin
McRae, he is the racer of
The day!

He
Is in
His
Allen Ford Focus
He'll crush the others
Like a
Colossal Diplodocus!

Roman Argent (8)
St Peter's CE (VC) Junior School, Marlborough

Sadness

Sadness is
The sound of rain
Coming down from the skies
Sadness is the fate of the world
Twisted up in lies, sadness is the colour
Of tears cried a million times, sadness is lifted
For a price that can't be bought by dimes
Sadness is when the heart is broken
And no one comes along, but no
One ever expects the sad
Heartbroken song.

Daynah Owen (10) & Paige Phillips (11)
St Peter's CE (VC) Junior School, Marlborough

Happiness

The colour of happiness is multicoloured like a rainbow.
Happiness feels like a warm blanket of snow.
Happiness is just like eating chocolate on a busy day
after work or school.
Happiness sounds like a first Christmas for everyone,
with a warm feeling inside.
Happiness looks like a warm, big smile from someone you love.
Happiness reminds me of spending time
with my family and friends.
Oh what great happiness!

Cameron Davies (11)
St Peter's CE (VC) Junior School, Marlborough

Honey

Honey is the honey hive
Making all the honey.
Who is the culprit stinging all the humans?
Can you guess who?
1, 2, 3, 4, 5 if you have not guessed right
Guess with all your might
Or turn this page upside down.

Answer: A bee.

Vita Linnane (8)
St Peter's CE (VC) Junior School, Marlborough

Terror

Terror is like a dark, cold, blue rock.
Terror feels as if there's a deep hole inside you,
It sounds like a soft whisper whispering, 'Help,'
It tastes like a painful burn at the back of my throat,
It looks like a life ending at a halt.
Terror reminds us of everything bad
But makes us look forward.

Iwan Parry-Evans (11)
St Peter's CE (VC) Junior School, Marlborough

The Lady Of Shalott - Part 4
(Inspired by 'The Lady of Shalott' by Alfred Lord Tennyson)

The knight stopped at the castle wall
Where the knight saw that someone tall,
On his way to Camelot.
The knight called out and climbed the wall,
'Your mirror is gone,' he called.
'She's pretty,' said Sir Lancelot.

She saw the brown horse gallop off,
Leaning on her chair that was soft,
Saw the Lady of Shalott.
'Again he started singing clear,
Just like drinking a cup of beer,'
Said the Lady of Shalott.

She heard a loving whisper clear,
'Is that Sir Lancelot I hear?
Hang on, wait, Sir Lancelot.'
She ran down at a speedy tide,
Then she saw the lovely outside,
At last there was Camelot.

Hannah Chapman (9)
Sheddingdean Community Primary School, Burgess Hill

The Princess Of The Time After Day

I meet her in a ballroom, what a great friend,
She dances with the gods and goddesses until the music ends.
She realises the time and sings lullabies
To drive the sun from the sky.

She leaves the room with a jolly smile,
The music then ends for a while.
She wears a long, black, wavy dress,
It's covered in stars and does not look a mess.

Her shiny dark hair
Goes everywhere.
Her beauty makes the stars go bright,
Her eyes make the moon sigh with jealousy.

She moves like a swan
Into the empty sky.
She stretches right out
In a blink of an eye.

A lovely face,
So calm and still,
Astronomers are blinded,
She is so beautiful.

As the sun now creeps in,
She tiptoes away, a happy thing.
She goes back to her favourite place in the world,
Again she dances with the gods and girls.

The princes of the time after day,
The greatest person, I have to say.
We're forever friends,
Right to the end
For eternity!

Jessica Green (11)
Sheddingdean Community Primary School, Burgess Hill

The Lady Of Shalott - Part 4
(Inspired by 'The Lady of Shalott' by Alfred Lord Tennyson)

Out of the big window she cried,
Lancelot heard and looked to spy.
Around the huge castle, dark skies,
All the flowers started to die,
Leading to Camelot.
Falling down to the crooked floor,
'Help,' whispering and crying more.
The wind blew open the brown door.
The Lady of Shalott.

Riding down to the lady's room,
To help the lady in her doom,
Happily walking, a nice groom
Arrived not a moment too soon
To save the Lady of Shalott.
'Shalott, let's go to a wizard.'
The lady felt like a blizzard.
Wizard gave a lizard drink to . . .
The Lady of Shalott.

She and Lancelot fell in love,
Their favourite bird was a dove,
A full moon was shining above,
Lancelot gave his knight a glove,
Colour came down from Camelot.
The curse was broken by Lancelot,
Lancelot kissed Lady Shalott.
They got married at Camelot,
She said, 'Love you lots, Lancelot.'

They were happily together,
Hopefully almost forever,
They would be there for each other,
Soon the lady was a mother,
Happy dad, he as Lancelot.
They lived happily ever after,
They were a mother and father.
Their cute child's name was Arthur.
The Lady of Shalott.

Tayla Lay (10)
Sheddingdean Community Primary School, Burgess Hill

The Lady Of Shalott - Part 4
(Inspired by 'The Lady of Shalott' by Alfred Lord Tennyson)

The brave knight hears the mirror crack
As the tower tumbles back
As it goes to Camelot
It goes from side to side
As the river is wide
On the island of Shalott.

The tumbled tower floats away
As the Lady of Shalott she sways
As she worries about Sir Lancelot
As she sways you can hear her say,
'I would love this night for my wedding day
To be married in Camelot.'

As she floats she says goodbye
People who see her give a sigh
As she travels to Camelot
She turns into stone
We all moan
On the way to Camelot.

Curtis Pummell (10)
Sheddingdean Community Primary School, Burgess Hill

The Lady Of Shalott - Part 4
(Inspired by 'The Lady of Shalott' by Alfred Lord Tennyson)

Sir Lancelot went to the tower
After the journey that was an hour,
Sir Lancelot had brought a flower
And he thought he had the power
To rescue Miss Shalott.
And the windows began to close,
Lady of Shalott began to moan
And she suddenly started to groan,
She couldn't see Camelot.

He then cut down all of the trees
And then down fell a pile of leaves,
And all of a sudden he saw
All of the bruises on his knees,
Bruises from Camelot.
Lancelot stood on the cold floor,
He started to kick down the door,
Then he slipped over an apple core,
He went to Miss Shalott.

'My dear lady, will you marry me?
It's the right decision, you'll see.
Oh please, my lady, you must agree,
We'll live forever happily,'
Said great Sir Lancelot.
Lancelot's heart was not broken.
Yes,' Lady of Shalott had spoken.
Hooray, the curse was now broken,
She went to Camelot.

All the years had now passed throughout
Lancelot's happiness was out,
Then Lancelot began to shout,
'Lady of Shalott, you should move out!
Now leave great Camelot.'

She left and looked for his arrow,
She found it in the wheelbarrow,
She shot herself with the arrow.
Bye, Lady of Shalott.

Hannah Elston (9)
Sheddingdean Community Primary School, Burgess Hill

The King Of Darkness

In my dream
I met on the moon, the king of night
In his cave of darkness fright.
His home of nightmares surrounds you in all,
He is the king of all those beastly bats.

His head shaped like the great moon,
His eyes like stars from above,
His cape of darkness all in one,
With his hood of invisibility.

He slumps onto his dazzling horse
Which gallops down to Earth with the stars.
It dodges all the meteors that meander through space,
Then it breaks through the atmosphere of the Earth
And appears on Earth like a curse.

Now his evil plans should start
As he watches the children,
Like a bird watching its prey.
He spooks the children with his vicious images,
While they snuggle in bed with their teds.

For now he goes back to his cave on the moon,
With all his beasts and bats.
We are not sure when he will come again,
But we hope it's not any time soon.

Kelly Blamire (11)
Sheddingdean Community Primary School, Burgess Hill

The Lady Of Shalott - Part 4
(Inspired by 'The Lady of Shalott' by Alfred Lord Tennyson)

Locked up in a beautiful room,
With not a single loom,
'What should I do?
I am doomed!'
Said the Lady of Shalott.

'The castle is shaking
And breaking,
There is a flood
With lots of mud,'
Cried the Lady of Shalott.

'The king has turned to dust,
And I will too.
I'm going to jump out the window,
And . . . here I gooooo, oh no!'
Said the Lady of Shalott.
'I went into the river.'
Then sighed.
'Sir Lancelot looked at me,'
Said the Lady of Shalott.

'I have only got an hour!'
'I will give you power.'
'I will sing louder!'
'Tirra-lira, tirra-lira!'
Sang Sir Lancelot.
Turning into dust,
Running *clip-clop,*
Dying into dust,
The Lady of Shalott.

Jade Conticelli (10)
Sheddingdean Community Primary School, Burgess Hill

The Lady Of Shalott - Part 4
(Inspired by 'The Lady of Shalott' by Alfred Lord Tennyson)

'The curse I fear is now on me,
I hope one day I will be free.'
The horse's bell rang merrily,
The castle was so lovely to see,
Looking at Camelot.
She had looked at the handsome knight,
With his new armour glowing bright,
On his way going off to fight,
It was Sir Lancelot.

She wondered who did the dreadful deed,
Her rotten father, the dead old reed?
Could it be the wicked witch who'd
Given her the poisonous food?
Thought the Lady of Shalott.
Looking, what a beautiful sight,
With all the rare birds taking flight,
Shadows casting eerie lights,
Looking at Camelot.

She saw a knight go riding by,
Close to the golden fields of rye
That met the cloudless, bright blue sky,
Which lit the loom where it lie.
She looked at Camelot.
Feeling her death day cometh,
She knew she'd soon just be a myth,
So she jumped off the high white cliff,
Goodbye, Lady of Shalott.

Hollie Steward (10)
Sheddingdean Community Primary School, Burgess Hill

The Lady Of Shalott
(Inspired by 'The Lady of Shalott' by Alfred Lord Tennyson)

A flash of light,
She screamed with fright,
In the starry night,
'Twas a horrible sight,
Of the Lady of Shalott.
The knight heard her scream,
Then he saw the steam.
He was very keen
To climb the walls of Shalott.

He called for a barge
That was very large,
He shouted to charge
To his horse called Marj.
He saw the mirror
In the fast-flowing river.
His spine gave a shiver
On the way to Camelot.

The red cross Knight
Had second sight,
Saw the lady with hr fright
In the starry night.
Saw sad Sir Lancelot
She was dead,
Nearly wed,
'Oh dear, one more funeral,' said
Sir Lancelot.

Elysia Paine (10)
Sheddingdean Community Primary School, Burgess Hill

The Lady Of Shalott · Part 4
(Inspired by 'The Lady of Shalott' by Alfred Lord Tennyson)

When the small mirror cracked she saw
A shining, golden, closed door
That led down to Camelot.
But before she could open the door,
Out came a blinded, crazy boar,
The monster of Shalott.

She picked up the needle from the floor,
Threw it at the beast at the door,
It fell to Lancelot.
His sword whistled fast through the air,
Off came the head of the big boar,
That was killed in Shalott.

Down came the lady in fear,
She could see Lancelot clear,
Beautiful Lancelot.
Thanked him did she and quickly kissed,
Just to find the amazing fist
Of Miss Lancelot.

She stuck to page boys, fit and young,
That smelt of really smelly dung,
Who lived in Camelot.
She lived a really happy life
Until she was murdered with a knife,
The Lady of Shalott.

Joseph Anderson (10)
Sheddingdean Community Primary School, Burgess Hill

The Lady Of Shalott
(Inspired by 'The Lady of Shalott' by Alfred Lord Tennyson)

She felt upset about her loom,
As her tears fled around the room.
She was cross with Camelot.
She looked out of the window clear,
Her heart beat faster, full of fear,
The Lady of Shalott.

Sir Lancelot rode to her castle,
With a special parcel.
Here came Sir Lancelot.
Sir Lancelot knocked down the door,
She fell dead on the floor.
The Lady of Shalott.

He picked her up off the floor,
He took her out of the door,
Well done, Sir Lancelot.
He carried her to the drawbridge,
Where her body was hid.
Poor Lady of Shalott.

Hannah Goldsmith (10)
Sheddingdean Community Primary School, Burgess Hill

Baby

A potty-needer
A cry-maker
A dummy-sucker
A Teletubbies-watcher
A bottle-user
A mummy-wanter
A milk-drinker
A nightmare-creator!

Jamie Bowles (11)
Sheddingdean Community Primary School, Burgess Hill

The Lady Of Shalott - Part 4
(Inspired by 'The Lady of Shalott' by Alfred Lord Tennyson)

She looked to Camelot once more,
It turned her very badly poor,
But there was no more Camelot.
Crying out with deadly tears,
'What's that I can hear in my ear
Running with life and fear?'
It was Sir Lancelot.

She looked into this knight's eyes,
He really was a great prize,
A knight of the realm,
Standing tall at the helm,
Floating down to Camelot.

She joined Lancelot in his boat,
And together in love they floated
Down to Camelot.
But before they could be wed,
Just as the curse had said,
She died in Camelot.

Blake Hayes (10)
Sheddingdean Community Primary School, Burgess Hill

What Is Red?

Red is for Manor Field,
A school so cool.
Red is for leaves,
Red as can be,
Swaying in the mild summer breeze.
Red is for an apple
Ripening in the sun.

Katie Watson (9)
Sheddingdean Community Primary School, Burgess Hill

The Lady Of Shalott - Part 4
(Inspired by 'The Lady of Shalott' by Alfred Lord Tennyson)

When she wakes, she's always weary
Her life is always so dreary
The river flows down to Camelot
Always the sky is blue
She just wants to shout, 'Yahoo!'
The Lady of Shalott.

'I'm coming to rescue my love
You're as beautiful as the sky above,'
Says Sir Lancelot
'The castle walls are white
But I'm going to fight
For my love,' says Sir Lancelot.

'The moon is as white as your hair
You don't look like a grizzly bear
You walk down to Camelot
The stars are very white
Do they give you a fright?'
Says Sir Lancelot.

Ben Docherty (10)
Sheddingdean Community Primary School, Burgess Hill

What Is Pink?

Pink is like a rose by a palace,
Pink is like a prawn that you eat,
Pink is like a diamond that shines in the sun,
Pink is like a pig who rolls in the mud,
Pink is like pink champagne that you drink,
Fizzy and bubbly too.

Bradley Birch (9)
Sheddingdean Community Primary School, Burgess Hill

The Phantom's Visit

The Hound of Hell is a nasty thing
It comes alive at night,
It dashes on a shadow's wing,
Sneaking in the landing light.

The Hound of Hell's breath is in my hair,
I keep my eyes shut tight,
The Hound of Hell's breath is everywhere,
Unseen in pale moonlight.

The Hound of Hell munches on children's dreams,
It fills them with dread,
It growls at its evil schemes
And traps them in my head.

The Hound of Hell is like an evil demon,
It breathes fire in the air, it scratches everything,
It spits!
It's midnight that I hate the most,
The hour my phantom visits.

Ollie Gregory (9)
Sheddingdean Community Primary School, Burgess Hill

Fire Engine

Water guzzler
Noise maker
Red wearer
Siren screamer
Life saver
Hero carrier
Tool transporter
Diesel gulper
Fire killer
Smoke extinguisher.

Jack Heckels & Justin Smith (11)
Sheddingdean Community Primary School, Burgess Hill

The Lady Of Shalott - Part 4
(Inspired by 'The Lady of Shalott' by Alfred Lord Tennyson)

Her life was sad without her loom,
She sat and cried in her dark room,
Poor Lady of Shalott.
Out the window a flash of light,
She screamed with fright and with might.
It flowed down to Camelot.

She knew her doom was coming soon
As she saw the pretty plume,
Poor Lady of Shalott.
She climbed down to the river
As she felt a little shiver,
Then came Sir Lancelot.

As she was on the ledge,
She went right to the edge,
Looking down to Camelot.
She took her last breath,
She fell down to her death.
Poor Lady of Shalott.

Charlotte Ingleton (10)
Sheddingdean Community Primary School, Burgess Hill

The Lady Of Shalott - Part 4
(Inspired by 'The Lady of Shalott' by Alfred Lord Tennyson)

She picked up the big mirror
Threw it in the crystal river
Following to Camelot
As the mirror got bigger
The mirror got nearer
Saw Sir Lancelot

She jumped to the ground
And she made a great sound
Saw Sir Lancelot
Red-crossed knight had a fright
All day and all of the night
Looking down to Camelot

As beautiful Shalott lay
Sleeping in the new-mown hay
Saw Sir Lancelot
Blood from her lovely head
Sadly she was dead
Floating down to Camelot.

Thomas Booth (10)
Sheddingdean Community Primary School, Burgess Hill

The Lady Of Shalott - Part 4
(Inspired by 'The Lady of Shalott' by Alfred Lord Tennyson)

The mirror cracks even more
Then a spirit comes through the door
'Look down at Camelot,'
Says the spirit, 'You will die.'
'I can see my life flying by,
I'm going to say goodbye to Lancelot!'

Lady of Shalott goes away
Sadly this is now her last day
She says goodbye to Camelot
That day she stands by the river
Having quite a freezing shiver
Saying goodbye to Shalott.

That day she goes to the river
Stands at the edge all a-quiver
Saying 'bye to Camelot
Then she takes her last breath
Then she knows she is near death
She has now lost Shalott.

Sammy Smith (10)
Sheddingdean Community Primary School, Burgess Hill

The Lady Of Shalott · Part 4
(Inspired by 'The Lady of Shalott' by Alfred Lord Tennyson)

Near the window which made her shiver
In her room looking at the river
Which led to Camelot
Then she looked at the sky
It was very high
While she was at Shalott

At this very midnight hour
Sir Lancelot was in his power
While she sat at Camelot
She jumped into the river and picked up a quiver
And swam to Camelot

Swam and said, 'This is freezing'
She was tired while wheezing
Swam up to Camelot
She swam until she froze
In the river she found her toes
Goodbye, the Lady of Shalott.

Toby Wardrobe (10)
Sheddingdean Community Primary School, Burgess Hill

Window

From my window I can see
Lots of colourful, pretty flowers.
I can see lots of busy people
Going for another busy day at work.
I can see long, wavy grass
As green as a tree.
I can see a tree as big as a building
And it's very green.
From my window I can hear
Very noisy builders building a house.
I can hear lots of pretty birds
Singing in the distance.
I can hear lots of cars
Going past in a rush.
The view from my window
Makes me feel happy because
It helps me get to sleep at night.

Sean Mallin (8)
Sheddingdean Community Primary School, Burgess Hill

Red Is . . .

Red is a tomato, big and juicy,
A pile of blood, slimy and sticky,
A fire engine blowing its siren,
A ruby, shining in the darkest cave,
A lava fountain splashing out of a volcano,
An apple as shiny as the sun,
A postbox, tall and thin,
A post van, short and fat,
A post office sorting letters, big and small,
A bottle of red wine, slippery and slimy,
A strawberry, large and ripe.

Siân Johnston (9)
Sheddingdean Community Primary School, Burgess Hill

Window

From my window I can see a cherry blossom tree
That is nearly as tall as my house.
I can see some really noisy birds
That are quite relaxing to me.
Sometimes I can see a nice ice cream man
Going down the road.
I can see lots of beautiful houses with people walking.
From my window I can hear people walking
And maybe running down my road.
I can hear noisy motorbikes on other roads.
I can hear noisy aeroplanes flying high in the sky.
The view from my window makes me feel happy
And calm all the time with my family
In my sweet and beautiful house.

Sarah Chapman (8)
Sheddingdean Community Primary School, Burgess Hill

The Lady Of Shalott · Part 4
(Inspired by 'The Lady of Shalott' by Alfred Lord Tennyson)

She fainted on the castle floor
As her reflection was no more.
Old Lady of Shalott.
Sir Lancelot cut down the trees
And on a hanger found the keys.
Entered Sir Lancelot.

He took her down to the river,
The cold wind made her skin shiver,
Poor Lady of Shalott.
A kiss upon her lips he made,
Her wrinkled face began to fade,
Brave knight, Sir Lancelot.

Prissy Parker (10)
Sheddingdean Community Primary School, Burgess Hill

Window

From my window I can see a pretty blossom
With white, floaty petals.
I can see bright orange street lamps
Shining through the window.
I can see my neighbour, Sophie,
And she is playing with her dog, Max.
From my window I can hear
Noisy birds tweeting.
I can hear cars zooming around all day long.
I can hear noisy bikes revving their engines.
The view from my window makes me feel
Happy, excited and sometimes tired.
I like spending time in my nice, beautiful house.

Emily Parsons (8)
Sheddingdean Community Primary School, Burgess Hill

Window

From my window I can see
The electrifying telephone wire and pole.
I can see the bright blue sky
And the great big clouds.
I can see my old tennis court in Haywards Heath.
I can see the old St Francis Hospital.
From my window I can hear aeroplanes
Shooting from airports and off in the air.
I can hear the TV on as loud as it will go.
I can hear the blackbirds tweeting in their nests.
The view from my window makes me feel
Like I want to go outside and
See what's going on.

Adam Tubbs (8)
Sheddingdean Community Primary School, Burgess Hill

The Phantom's Visit

The fire demon is a horrible thing,
It comes alive at night.
It creeps in on shadow's wing,
Glowing in the landing light.

The fire demon's breath is in my hair,
I keep my eyes shut tight.
The fire demon's breath is everywhere,
Unseen in pale moonlight.

The fire demon feeds on children's dreams,
It seals them with dread,
It laughs at its evil schemes
And throws them in my head.

Joshua Plank (9)
Sheddingdean Community Primary School, Burgess Hill

Window

From my window I can see my
Colourful guinea pigs in their cages.
I can see my bright orange swing,
I can see a clear blue pond,
I can see a big brown bird table.
From my window I can hear
The beautiful sound of the birds,
I can hear my granny
Catching my cheeky guinea pigs,
I can hear my dad noisily banging in the shed.
The view from my window
Makes me feel like I'm alive.

Charlotte Brown (8)
Sheddingdean Community Primary School, Burgess Hill

The Scary Ghost Visit

The mysterious ghost
Is a mean old thing,
It comes alive at night.
It floats in shadow's wing,
It stays in the landing light.

The cold breath is in my hair,
I keep my eyes shut tight,
Unseen in the pale moonlight,
The ghost treads on children's dreams.

It fills them with dread,
It howls at its evil schemes.

Bryony Tarrant (9)
Sheddingdean Community Primary School, Burgess Hill

Burning Fire

A wood destroyer
A human cooker
A night lighter
A forest eater
A noise creator
A bug attracter
A smoke maker
An ice cap melter
A dream building
An eye attracter
An armed killer.

Owain McLoughlin (11)
Sheddingdean Community Primary School, Burgess Hill

Dog

Deep sleeper
Daydreamer
House guarder
Four-legged walker
Bark maker
Toy chewer
Ball catcher
Life saver
Gate leaper
Man befriender.

Jaime Pink (10)
Sheddingdean Community Primary School, Burgess Hill

God

Life giver
Home maker
World creator
Angel leader
People watcher
Universe ruler
Evil destroyer
Sin forgiver
World improver
Devil hater.

Paige Walker-Pettit (10)
Sheddingdean Community Primary School, Burgess Hill

Bedtime Dreaming!

It's five to seven, it's time for bed,
I'm tired, I'm tired.
Ideas are swirling round my head,
I'm too tired, I've got to go upstairs.
My arms are hurting but I've got to comb my hair,
I've got to clean my teeth and have a wash with soap.
My legs are bleeding, my back is killing, I really just can't cope.
I try to go to sleep,
But my younger sister keeps a creak.
When I hear it I get frightened
So I slip under the covers to pretend.
I turn around going *creep, creep, creep.*
Then I see someone, oh what shall I do? I really need to sleep.
I think, *who could that be? Maybe a mister?*
I get out of bed, phew, it is only my sister.
Down the staircase carefully, not making a sound,
I go into the bathroom seeing if anyone's around.
I see a spider which I don't like much either,
I am looking forward to a good night's sleep,
Now I don't hear my sister creep.
But I wake up frightened to death,
What if I fall back to sleep
With another dream where I hear another creak?
Now it's all quiet,
I lie in bed and rest.
I put my head down on the pillow,
Cuddling my teddies is the best!

Hana-Jo Chester (9)
The Queen Anne Royal Free CE (C) First School, Windsor

My Amazing Cat

My cat
Has a fluffy mat.
She likes to purr,
With fluffy fur.
My cat loves to jump
With a hump.
She loves fish
Without a dish.
My favourite part
Is her heart.
My cat is cute,
She hates the sound of a flute.
She climbs trees
And chases bees.
I love my cat,
My cat loves me!

Premleen Kaur Virdi (8)
The Queen Anne Royal Free CE (C) First School, Windsor

My Hairdo

I look cool with my new hairdo,
It's all new and blue.
I wonder what my teachers will say and do.
I think I will shape it like the moon,
Maybe I'll be as famous as Wayne Roo.

Daniel Wren
The Queen Anne Royal Free CE (C) First School, Windsor

Spring

Spring is many colours, from emerald green and soft pinks
To dark brown oak and the sun's bright yellow,
It reminds me of fluffy little lambs skipping about
In a lush, green field.
It sounds like a tuneful melody
With the birds singing in the trees,
It smells like pollen with the sweet scent
Of blossom filling the air,
It looks peaceful with bright sun smiling down
On the rain-jewelled grass,
Twinkling underneath the trees laden with
Delicate pink and white blossom
Swaying in the calm breeze.
Bright flowers with smooth petals are
Lined up neatly around the border of your garden.

Isobel Gatehouse (11)
The Stoke Poges School, Slough

Sadness

It looks like people looking sad,
It sounds like people crying,
Its colour is grey.
It makes you feel very lonely,
It smells dank and like smoke,
It tastes like a soggy tear,
It reminds me of when my grandma
Had a brain haemorrhage
That also caused a stroke.

Reah Mann (10)
The Stoke Poges School, Slough

Winter

Winter reminds me of freshly laid snow,
Winter makes me feel cold,
Winter smells of burning wood,
Winter tastes of freshly-cooked turkey,
Winter looks like a really big Christmas tree,
Winter sounds like kids throwing snowballs,
Winter is as white as snow.

Idris Hussain (10)
The Stoke Poges School, Slough

Summer

Summer reminds me of being away from school for six weeks,
It sounds like lawnmowers cutting the grass,
It looks like a red back where the sun's burnt it,
It smells like freshly cut grass and nature of the trees.
There are all sorts of colours: red, yellow and orange.
It feels like the warm sun,
It tastes of barbecued chicken.

Ethan Relf (10)
The Stoke Poges School, Slough

Excitement

Excitement is like a smile,
Excitement feels like happiness,
Excitement smells like a big bag of presents,
Excitement sounds of laughing,
Excitement reminds me of being happy,
Excitement is the colour of sparkly yellow.

Aais Bukhari (8)
The Stoke Poges School, Slough

Fear

Fear smells like a dark, dark wood,
Fear is the colour of blood dripping on the ground below,
Fear reminds me of a dark, dry land,
Fear looks like a dark playground,
Fear sounds like people screaming,
Fear feels like monsters' teeth and jaws.

Saba Iqbal (8)
The Stoke Poges School, Slough

Pain!

Pain sounds like an agonising scream,
Red is the colour of pain.
Pain reminds me of when I fell down the stairs.
Pain looks like a savage beast,
Pain feels like a bloody tear in your flesh,
Pain smells of blood and misery.

Cameron David (11)
The Stoke Poges School, Slough

Joy

Joy reminds me of children playing in the bright, hot sun,
Joy smells of lovely lavender,
Joy's colour is yellow, like some stars,
Joy feels like having fun with friends in the swimming pool,
Joy sounds like happy animals playing,
Joy looks fun, like eating ice cream.

Charlotte Ashley (8)
The Stoke Poges School, Slough

Anger

Anger feels like hot, breathing fire,
Anger sounds like shouting and screaming,
Anger is dark red,
Anger looks like hot, boiling lava,
Anger smells of smoking steam,
Anger reminds me of fighting.

Suzilah Chowdhary (8)
The Stoke Poges School, Slough

Friendship

Friendship is the colour orange,
Friendship looks like an orange flying pig,
Friendship sounds very loud and joyful,
Friendship tastes of a hot, buttered fig,
Friendship smells of freshly cut grass,
Friendship feels like a smooth, warm flask.

Daniel Nankivell (11)
The Stoke Poges School, Slough

Love

Love feels like a flower that has just bloomed,
Love smells like a beautiful rose,
Love reminds me of my teddy bear,
Love looks like a person kissing another,
Love is the colour of a beating heart,
Love sounds like someone munching on chocolate.

Emily Shieldhouse (7)
The Stoke Poges School, Slough

Surprise!

Surprise reminds you of happiness,
Surprise smells sweet and sour,
Surprise feels soft but tough,
Surprise looks like someone blushing,
Surprise is coloured red as red can be,
A colour of sweetness and shock.

Gurneet Brar (11)
The Stoke Poges School, Slough

Happiness

It reminds me of good times,
It's as yellow as the sun,
It feels like joy in your body,
People cheering as they've passed,
It smells like a hot cake,
It looks like a reward.

Gionluca Mallia (11)
The Stoke Poges School, Slough

Pain

Pain reminds me of someone pushing me,
Pain is like stinky feet,
Pain reminds me of red blood,
Pain feels like a dog biting me,
Pain looks like I am going to fall,
Pain sounds like big waves hurting me.

Sabah Mahmood (8)
The Stoke Poges School, Slough

Silence

Silence sounds like a butterfly's wings beating in the sun,
Silence feels like the calm ocean,
Silence reminds me of my soft bed,
Silence has the colour of the frozen glass in the window,
Silence smells like the cold air around us,
Silence looks like 29 hardworking children!

Anastasia Bergman (7)
The Stoke Poges School, Slough

Excitement

Excitement sounds like children playing football,
Excitement smells of ribs on a barbecue,
Excitement feels like good things,
Excitement looks like a really good thing,
Excitement reminds me of happy times,
Excitement is like a rainbow.

Ethan Short (8)
The Stoke Poges School, Slough

Fear

Fear smells like sweat,
Fear reminds me of a cold, dark corridor,
Fear is as black as a blank face,
Fear sounds like a trembling mouth,
Fear is like a big scary monster.

Tayyib Fazal (8)
The Stoke Poges School, Slough

Winter

What does it sound like?
Winter is very windy.
Winter - cold and windy.
Winter reminds me of snow.
Winter, it is so cold.

Ismail Mehmood (8)
The Stoke Poges School, Slough

The South & South West

Young Writers Information

We hope you have enjoyed reading this book - and that you will continue to enjoy it in the coming years.

If you like reading and writing poetry drop us a line, or give us a call, and we'll send you a free information pack.

Alternatively if you would like to order further copies of this book or any of our other titles, then please give us a call or log onto our website at www.youngwriters.co.uk.

Young Writers Information
Remus House
Coltsfoot Drive
Peterborough
PE2 9JX
(01733) 890066

All aboard the Poetry Express!

It's time to depart on a fantastic journey of poetic discovery. Our passengers are our talented young writers driven only by their imagination. As they progress on their journey, they overcome the challenges of simile, personification and rhyme to become masters of verse. Along the way they encounter dragons, unicorns, pirates and monsters, so you'd better watch out!

With free verse, cinquains and haikus all featuring as stops on the Poetry Express, you'll find there's something for everyone to enjoy. We're sure you'll agree that this adventure is one you'll want to join, so why not hop on!

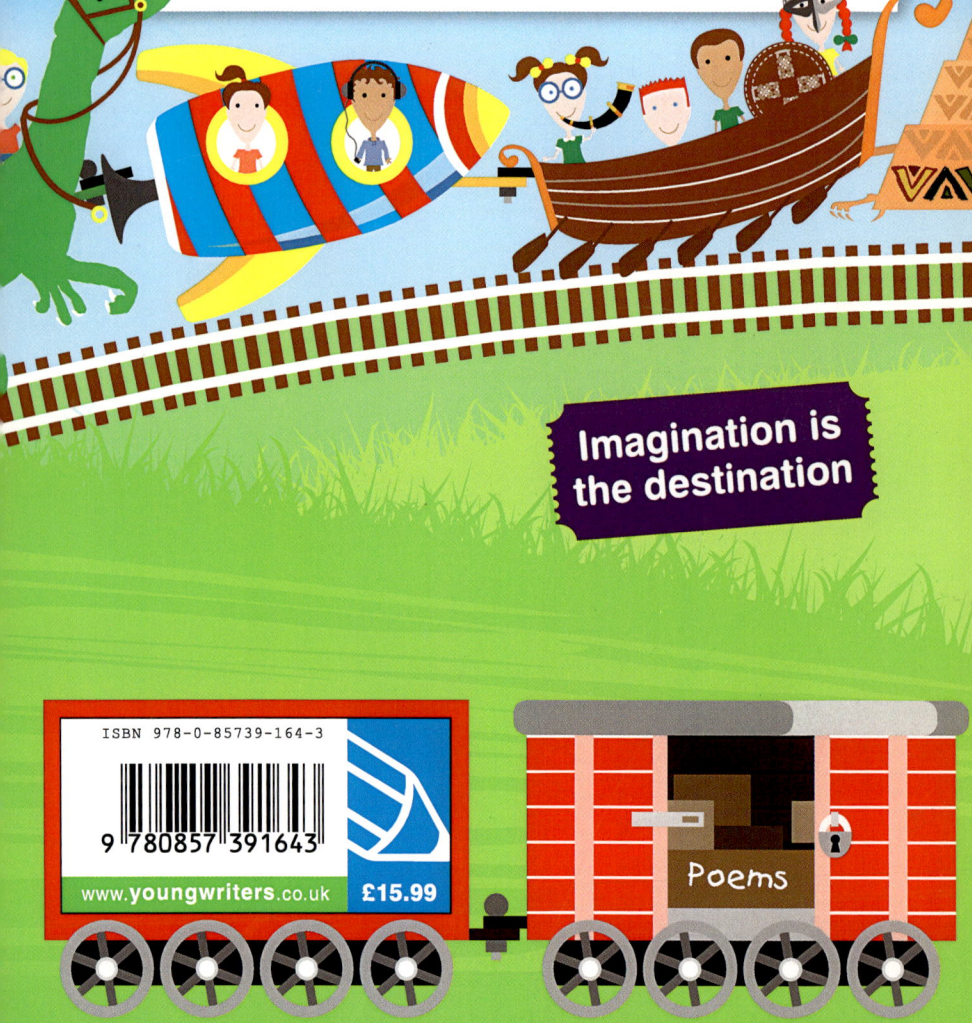

Imagination is the destination

ISBN 978-0-85739-164-3

www.youngwriters.co.uk   £15.99

Poems